History Is Wrong

ERICH VON DÄNIKEN

History Is Wrong

Translated by Nicholas Quaintmere

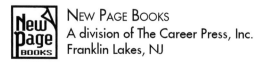
NEW PAGE BOOKS
A division of The Career Press, Inc.
Franklin Lakes, NJ

HISTORY IS WRONG
EDITED BY JODI BRANDON
TYPESET BY EILEEN MUNSON
Cover design by Howard Grossman / 12E Design
Printed in the U.S.A. by Courier

To order this title, please call toll-free 1-800-CAREER-1 (NJ and Canada: 201-848-0310) to order using VISA or MasterCard, or for further information on books from Career Press.

The Career Press, Inc., 3 Tice Road, PO Box 687,
Franklin Lakes, NJ 07417
www.careerpress.com
www.newpagebooks.com

Library of Congress Cataloging-in-Publication Data
Däniken, Erich von, 1935–
    History is wrong / by Erich von Däniken.
        p. cm.
    Includes index.
    ISBN 978-1-60163-086-5
        1. Civilization, Ancient—Extraterrestrial influences. 2. Life on other planets. I. Title.

CB156.D3323 2009
001.942--dc22

                                                                2009024184

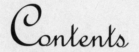

Contents

Mysterious
Books

An Unusual Question

My quick survey only took a couple of days. I started with my wife, the apple of my eye, and continued at the office. I asked everyone the same question. Then I called some of my relatives and later—feeling a little pluckier— even complete strangers in a restaurant. "Excuse me. Could I ask you a question?" I was polite—as one is—even though a lot of the guests simply wrinkled their brows in puzzlement, seemingly asking themselves, *What the hell does this guy want?* But in the end I had asked a hundred people, and that was enough.

"Have you ever heard of the Voynich manuscript?"

"The w-h-a-t?"

Out of one hundred people, only one had ever *heard* of the Voynich manuscript, and even then knew nothing of any consequence. Voynich manuscript? Wasn't there something about that in *P.M.* magazine in Germany?[1] Voynich? Some sort of secret code from the Second World War? A secret organization? Voynich? Voynich? Yet there are countless pages about the Voynich manuscript on the Internet, for instance at *www.voynich.nu,* a site that also features countless links to other sources. Hundreds of treatises have been written about the Voynich manuscript by both scientists and laymen alike, including books—one of the best by the Britons Kennedy and Churchill: *The Voynich Manuscript.*[2] It contains the entire history of this puzzling and crazy document, including much of the speculation and attempts at deciphering the text.

To be honest, just about everything that could be written about the Voynich manuscript has already been written, so it makes no sense to repeat it here. Nevertheless, there are still a few blank spots on the world map of Voynich scholarship—interconnections that I have never encountered in any of the literature about the Voynich manuscript. Our way of thinking—so we believe—is characterized by logic and information. In reality, we are just like the verses of an enormous book, from which we don't even know the first 4,000 pages.

We're living on a single page. And in terms of the entire composition, we know neither the vocabulary nor even the alphabet. Today's reason cannot accept the reason of the past. And in so saying, I turn to the people who have remained intelligent, even while being a part of academia. My readers shouldn't end up like the hundred people I had questioned earlier. So, for that reason, I'd like to tell you a little about the incredible Voynich manuscript.

The Man Behind the Manuscript

On October 31, 1865, in the city of Telšiai in Lithuania, the Wojnicz family was blessed by the arrival of a son. Records show that they christened him Michal, but he changed this in later life to Wilfryd. His father held a position in a government office and sent him first to school and then to university in Moscow, where he studied chemistry and qualified as a pharmacist. He became politically active, becoming involved with the Polish nationalist movement, which was fighting to liberate Poland from the Russians. He joined a group of young activists who were attempting to save two of their comrades from execution. This led to his arrest in 1885 and incarceration in solitary confinement in a Warsaw prison. In the summer of 1887, Wilfryd was to be transported to a prison camp in Siberia, but somehow he escaped and went on the run. He made his way—no one quite knows how—to London, where he resurfaced three years later.

Living in the London suburb of Chiswick, he met up with a group of fanatical Englishmen and exiled Russians bent on ending the rule of the czar. They published a revolutionary magazine called *Free Russia,* which Wilfrid Voynich (having anglicized his name) sold on the streets. With the help of his girlfriend, Ethel Boole, he worked his way up to becoming manager of a small bookshop. In September 1902, the two married—not purely for love, partially for convenience, as Wilfrid wanted to take on British nationality and he could only do this by marrying a British citizen.

Wilfrid Voynich led an exciting life with many ups and downs—and he was permanently short of money. Mr. and Mrs. Voynich began smuggling banned books to Russia, and Wilfrid lived in constant fear of becoming the victim of a political attack. So he traveled under a series of aliases—depending on which country he was in and what company he was keeping. Back in London, Voynich opened an antiquarian bookshop and began buying up old manuscripts and books. The shop was soon a chaotic treasure trove of exotic parchments and printed material from throughout the centuries. Of the discovery of the "most mysterious book in the world," Voynich claimed he had discovered it in an old castle in southern Europe.[3] The richly colored manuscript had lain hidden in an old chest and nobody had known of its existence. The entire work is written down on parchment and illustrated with countless color drawings, and he had immediately suspected that it was produced sometime in the second half of the 13th century.

Since that time, the unreadable work has been known as the Voynich manuscript.

What Happened Next

A while after Voynich's death (on March 19, 1931) it became known that his claim to have found the manuscript in an "old castle" was a fabrication. Wilfrid left behind a will in which he left the manuscript to his wife, Ethel, and his secretary, Anne Nill. After Ethel's death Anne Nill became the sole owner of the Voynich manuscript, and she confessed in a letter that was not to be published until after *her* death, that Wilfrid had found the manuscript in 1912 in a former Jesuit collegio, in the Villa Mandragone. This villa had been a Jesuit training center and had housed an impressive collection of old manuscripts from the library of the Collegium Romanum. In 1870, the Jesuits had feared that Vittorio Emanuel's soldiers might plunder the library to make themselves a bit of money, so the collection was transferred to the Villa

Mandragone in Frascati, north of Rome. This was where Voynich discovered the manuscript, while rummaging around in an old trunk. The Jesuits had needed money for restoration work to their ramshackle building and the brothers had readily offered the crafty bookseller from London cases full of yellowing manuscripts. Voynich purchased 30 old volumes and the Jesuits, who had thought themselves sly, never realized what a treasure they had pressed into Wilfrid Voynich's willing hands.

To an antiquarian like Wilfrid Voynich, who regularly dealt with piles upon piles of ancient texts, the curious, multicolored parchment in the heavy dark brown and matt-varnished trunk must have really leapt out and caught the eye. But what truly surprised him was a letter he found pressed between the front cover and the first page. This letter, composed in Latin, had been written by a certain "Johannes Marcus Marci de Cronland" in Prague and was dated August 19, 1666. It was addressed to his friend Athanasius Kircher and explained how he was sending him a work that no one could read. If anyone could decipher the text, he wrote, it would be Athanasius. On the origin of the manuscript, Marci wrote:

> Dr. Raphael, tutor in the Bohemian language to Ferdinand III, then King of Bohemia, told me the said book had belonged to the Emperor Rudolph and that he presented to the bearer who brought him the book 600 ducats. He believed the author was Roger Bacon, the Englishman.[4]

This is where the story starts getting complicated.

Emperor Rudolph II, crowned in 1576, was a melancholic man plagued by self-doubt and delusions who put great faith in astrologers and magicians, even sponsoring them with gifts of money. At that time, Prague, Rudolph's capital, was a center of secret societies, alchemists, and occultists. Prague was the city of the *golem,* a city where the Apocalypse (the "secret revelation" that follows the four gospels of the New Testament) was a frequent topic of daily conversation. The Voynich manuscript would have fit rather well into that period, shortly before the outbreak of the Thirty Years' War, as well as being something that would have appealed to the court of Rudolph II. Unfortunately, Marci had also noted in his letter to Athanasius that Emperor Rudolph also believed that the manuscript was the work of Roger Bacon.

The Bacon Connection

This "hot tip" must have electrified Wilfrid Voynich, as Roger Bacon (c. 1214–1294) was considered by many to be a universal genius. Bacon had studied in Oxford and taught philosophy in Paris. He was the author of numerous works, such as the *Opus maius,* the *Opus minus,* the *Opus tertium,* and a phenomenal encyclopedia. Bacon was way ahead of his time: he wrote about ships of the future that could be steered without a rudder and could be operated by a single man, and about fighting vehicles that could move themselves with incredible power. He also had a few things to say about flying, even back in 1256: "Flying machines (*instrumenta volandi*) will be constructed...they were manufactured before a time and it is certain that man will have an instrument to fly."[5]

Bacon, who also criticized the moral authority of the church, lived in dangerous times. After the publishing of his final work, *Compendium studii Theologiae,* Bacon was named Doctor Mirabilis for his linguistic and scientific achievement. Seemingly to show his conformity, he joined the Franciscan order, but very soon came into conflict with his superiors and was even placed under monastic arrest.

Is this same Roger Bacon who is supposed to be the author of the Voynich manuscript? There is no proof, but it can't be completely excluded as a possibility. A book of the scope of the Voynich manuscript, however, would have probably been too great a challenge—even for one as talented as Roger Bacon. After all, it contains a completely new alphabet, which defies all logic, and color illustrations of plants and utensils that existed nowhere in the world. On the other hand, Bacon must surely have had access to certain ancient texts; otherwise he could hardly have gone on about classical flying machines in his tract about the "secret arts."[6] These kinds of flying devices were indeed often mentioned in ancient documents.

The annals tell the tale of the Chinese king *Cheng Tang*, who owned "flying wagons"[7] that were not produced in his own workshops, but came from a distant folk called *Chi Kung*. This race lived 40,000 Li "beyond the Jade gate."[8] Wherever that was, it must have been at least halfway around the world, because one "Li" corresponded to 644.40 meters. (That makes 40,000 Li more than 25,000 kilometers!) Word for word, the *Chi Kung* people were described as follows:

> They could even manufacture flying wagons that, in a good wind, could cover great distances. In the time of *Tang* [around 1760 B.C.] the west wind brought such a wagon to *Yu-Chou (Honan)*, whereupon *Tang* destroyed it because he did not want his people to see such a thing.[9]

Chinese chronicler *Kuo P'o* (270–324 A.D.) picked up where his forebears left off, writing: "The intricate work of the fabulous *Chi Kung* people is truly admirable. Together with the wind, they have exerted their brains and invented a flying wagon which, climbing and sinking, depending on their path, brought guests to *Tang*."[10]

Flying machines such as these, although they may seem to us today a little bizarre, have been preserved in drawings and wall paintings. King *Cheng Tang* hid these ancient flyers from his subjects. His "chief engineer" *Ki Kung Shi* even managed to replicate one of the heavenly wagons, but the flying monstrosity was later destroyed to protect its secrets forever. Disarmament in ancient China! In his work *Shang hai ti-shing*, chronicler *Kuo P'o* tells of various occurrences that took place in that epoch.[11] His writings not only include reports on the flying wagons, but also describe flying wheels.

My short detour on ancient aviation was not made without reason. Did Roger Bacon know of texts such as these? Those who are acquainted with my books know that flying wagons appear in countless historical traditions; it's just that no one takes notice of them. Indian king *Rumanvat,* who reigned many thousand years ago, even had a massive sky ship built in which many groups of people could be transported at once.[12] In the Indian epics *Ramayana* and *Mahabharata* there are more than 50 passages that clearly describe flying machines,[13] and in the Ethiopian *Kebra Negast,* the Book of the Glory of Kings, the description of King Solomon's flying wagon even includes details of top speeds![14] And so on, and so on! Those who don't know these ancient texts about aviation should keep quiet. It seems to me that Roger Bacon must have known at least one of these old sources—and for that reason he didn't stay quiet at all.

All these ancient literary traditions from past epochs have a big problem (one of many!): only a handful of people know the texts. On top of that, countless thousands of books from the past no longer exist. The great library of Alexandria went up in flames in 47 A.D. and again in 391 A.D. The same happened with the libraries of Jerusalem, Pergamon, and many other great cities of antiquity where wars raged. And when Central America was conquered by the soldiers of the cross, the monks—in their holy fervor—burnt thousands of manuscripts written by the Maya and the Aztecs. All that antique knowledge—simply gone up in smoke! Where are the originals of texts like *Enoch, Solomon, Manetho,* and the like? Where are the original works about Atlantis? My little departure into the gulf of time reveals an insipid, unknowing society that passes judgment as if it actually knew something.

Off to the United States

Following his exciting find in the Villa Mandragone in Frascati, Wilfrid Voynich traveled to the United States in November 1914. He opened a small antiquarian bookshop and gave lectures to public and private circles. One person who was particularly impressed with the manuscript was philologist William Newbold, professor of Intellectual and Moral Philosophy at the

University of Pennsylvania. In 1919, Professor Newbold began an attempt to decipher the text, even though he only had access to a few pages of the manuscript. He quickly developed a theory that the Voynich manuscript contained microscopic characters that would only be revealed under extreme magnification. In a lecture he delivered on April 20, 1921, Newbold claimed he was able to translate the crude text. Unfortunately for him, he also believed that the manuscript had been written by Roger Bacon. Ten years later, Professor Newbold's decipherment was definitively debunked. There are no hidden characters in the Voynich manuscript, and Newbold's translation turned out to be just hot air: the wishful thinking of an academic who would dearly have loved to make history himself.

Wilfrid Voynich desperately needed money. He set the price of the manuscript at $160,000 and wasn't prepared to budge. He was left sitting holding a pile of colored parchments of uncertain heritage that no one could read and no one wanted to buy—a manuscript, let's not forget, with a blank cover, no title, and no author. By the time Wilfrid died in 1931, there was still no potential buyer in sight. He left the manuscript to his wife, Ethel, and his secretary, Anne Nill. Following Ethel's death, Nill finally managed to sell the pile of parchments to an antique book dealer from New York, Hans-Peter Kraus, for $24,500. Kraus put the price back up to same amount that Voynich had demanded, $160,000, and, like Voynich himself before him, wasn't willing to bargain. In 1969 Kraus finally donated the manuscript to Yale University, which is where it has remains to this day, in the Beinecke Rare Book and Manuscript Library with the catalog number "MS 408."

A Cryptographic Challenge

For nearly 80 years, countless specialists have tried their hand at unraveling the Voynich puzzle, including some of the world's best cryptographers, who would usually not have the slightest problem cracking any code. These specialists have analyzed the frequency of glyphs, compared them with hand-written texts from the 13th century, attempted to separate vowels from conso-nants. All in vain. Ulli Kulke, a science correspondent from the German journal *Die Welt*, covered one of the more recent attempts. He reported how British computer scientist Gordon Rugg had tried to use techniques from the 16th century to demonstrate that the manuscript was a fake. Rugg had used a table with 40 horizontal rows and 39 vertical columns containing various group-ings of Voynich characters. Afterward, he used a Cardan grille with three holes, which was moved about to display combinations of these characters. "The result was gibberish without any meaning whatsoever, but with the same inter-nal structure as the original text."[15]

The Voynich manuscript, however, consists of much more than just inde-finable syllables or "letters." There are also the colored drawings that are placed left or right on the parchment pages, often over and even in the middle of the text, as if the writing was describing the contents of the illustrations. So the next question for the experts has to be: Is it *really* all made up? Is it forgery or willful reverie of the kind that crops up every few years in one psychiatric clinic or other? In their excellent book about the Voynich manuscript, Kennedy and Churchill closely examine the best-established forgery theories without finding any conclusive answer.[16] Was the whole thing just some kind of religious delusion, a torrent of inner or—if you like—heavenly voices scribbled down onto parchment by some delusional fanatic caught in the grips of ecstasy? It's not unknown to hap-pen. Did some mad genius suddenly decide, *Now I'll leave the research-ers of the future some nut that they'll never be able to crack*? Could it really be Roger Bacon, the man with such great knowledge of past ages, who was behind it all? Bacon would have had various reasons for putting down his insights in a secret language—namely, keeping the clergy off his back. On the other hand, Bacon would never have produced anything that was indecipherable. It would have been enough for him that his critics, right up to the Pope himself, would be unable to read the text. He would have wanted his friends to know the key. But that would mean that there would have to be some kind of system hidden in the text somewhere. Today's cryptographers can crack just about any code—especially with the computing power that's available to them nowadays—but only if the text is based on a certain amount of symmetry or has a particular logical structure. This logic is missing entirely from the Voynich text. Or did Bacon copy the Voynich manuscript from a much older source that seemed to him to be important, although he couldn't understand a word? Are the words and pictures perhaps the work of some mystic intent on swindling King Rudolph II out of 600 ducats? That was a fortune back in those days. Or—and this is the layest idea—is Voynich himself the forger? It is no secret that he lived permanently beyond his means and always needed money. One of his contemporaries described Voynich as "capable and dynamic, but unbearably coarse and arrogant."[17] Nevertheless, Voynich himself cannot be a candidate, as it has been shown that the manuscript definitely existed before 1887.

Old, But How Old?

After all, what are modern dating methods for? The Voynich manuscript consists of leaves of parchment that have been written on and drawn upon using various inks and colors. Both the paper and the colors are organic, meaning they can be dated using C-14 dating techniques. Radiocarbon dating is a process that measures amount of decay of the carbon-14 isotope. The half-life of carbon-14 is known: after 5,600 years, half of the original amount of carbon-14 is gone; after 11,200 years, three quarters; and so on. The method isn't 100-percent flawless, as it assumes a constant level of atmospheric carbon-14. However, the amount of carbon in the air actually fluctuates quite considerably. On top of that, carbon-14 is not especially reliable for artifacts that are only a few centuries old. And finally, the current owner of the manuscript, Yale University, has steadfastly refused to make the document available for dating—for good reason. In 1965, Yale University acquired the so-called *Vinland Map,* a parchment mappa mundi depicting a large island to the west of Greenland in exactly the location of present-day Newfoundland. If genuine, it would prove that the Vikings had discovered North America. In 1972, however, during a chemical analysis of the ink used on the map, a team of scientists discovered that it contained a chemical substance that wasn't used in inks until the 20th century. This meant the map had to be a fake. Allegedly. Further tests, which were carried out at various intervals until 1995, provided conflicting results with controversial datings. The dispute has, to this day, not been resolved. For this reason, Yale University has declined to have the Voynich manuscript dated using the C-14 method.

Even if it were possible to date the manuscript, it still wouldn't mean an end to the controversy, as the question of the provenance of the text remains. To make it clearer: every devout Christian believes that the Bible contains the word of God, and, as far as the Gospels of the New Testament are concerned, the popular belief is that the companions of Jesus of Nazareth wrote down everything that the master said or did, in a sort of running chronicle. These chronicles were even given a name: *the urtexts.*

In fact, none of that is true. The often-quoted and, in terms of theological rabulistics, very fertile original texts don't even exist. What have we really got in our hands? Copies that were exclusively produced between the fourth and 10th centuries after Christ's death. And these copies, around 1,500 of them, are in themselves copies of copies; and not one single one of them completely concurs with any of the others. More than 80,000 (yes, *eighty thousand!*) deviations have been counted. There's not one single page of these so-called urtexts that doesn't contain one contradiction or other. Each new edition was the author's interpretation of the original verses rather than a direct copy, and was adapted to meet the needs and attitudes of the times. In the process, these biblical urtexts have amassed thousands of easily verifiable errors. The best-known of these texts, Codex Sinaiticus—like the Codex Vaticanus, written in the fourth century—was found in 1844 in the Monastery of Saint Catherine at the foot of Mount Sinai. It contains no less than 16,000 corrections (*sixteen thousand!*), which have been attributed to at least seven different editors. Some parts of the text have been corrected repeatedly and replaced with another piece of original text. Professor Friedrich Delitzsch, a top expert, found 3,000 copy errors in the text.[18]

What has all this got to do with the Voynich manuscript? I'll explain. Let's assume that the text and images are ancient. The content was copied onto parchment in some old hermit's cell without any changes being made to the text—because by this time no one understood the slightest thing about what the manuscript was actually about. Perhaps it was believed to be a holy text or other important lore that was only to be read by initiates or in the distant future. The only thing that was important to the assiduous copiers was to preserve the original content for later generations, perhaps because the existing manuscript had been eaten by moths and was beginning to decay. If this was the case then the manuscript would have no author. Even if the parchment and ink of the Voynich manuscript were only 200 years old, the age of the original content would remain a mystery. It is possible that a successful deciphering attempt will open up a precipice into ancient knowledge that will change the world (inasmuch as the zeitgeist will let it be changed!). David Kahn, an American cryptologist, predicts: the Voynich manuscript could be described as a bomb that will go off on the day that it is finally decoded.[19]

Curiouser and Curiouser

As far as the content of the Voynich manuscript is concerned, for the time being there is very little to be said. The script and the illustrations in the text are another thing entirely. They can, to a certain extent, be sorted into rough categories.

Folios 2–66 feature plants together with their flowers and confusing tangles of roots. Always accompanied by text.

The following folios, 63–73, are filled with astronomical depictions of stars, the sun, the moon, possible zodiacal signs, and naked women lying around in baths or bubbling out of tube-like openings.

The 10 pages that follow provide little in the way of optical clues for us today. I can't shake off the amateurish impression that they portray some kind of "health spa" or "fountain of youth," as the women depicted seem to be rising from some kind of colored liquid. The rest is an indecipherable mix of stars of differing sizes and colors, and in between is something that looks like an amulet and radiant flowers. Thirty-three folios are pure text, line after unreadable line.

The manuscript itself is made up of different-sized parchments, most of them around 23 by 15 centimeters. Curiously, the pages are numbered in a style typical of that used in the 16th century. Whoever the author or the scribe was, he seems to have been conversant with the ciphers of the time. The curves and strokes, embellishments reminiscent of shorthand, and "g"- and "o"-like loops do not seem to be comparable to any known alphabet, least of all Ancient Greek, Latin, or even Cyrillic. Despite all this, the longer I dwelled on the text the more I had a feeling that I had seen something similar in a completely different corner of the Earth. The story is turning somersaults and maybe my little contribution will help the cryptographers in some small way toward solving the riddle.

Artifacts in Ecuador

In Ecuador, the hot, tropical country straddling the equator in South America, there is a small town called Cuenca. There is a church there that carries the name *Maria Auxiliadora,* which translates roughly as "the helpful mother of God." For 50 years, the Catholic diocese was looked after by a certain Father Carlo Crespi.

Father Crespi displaying some of the treasures from his collection.

He enjoyed a reputation as a friend of the Indios, and even during his lifetime the folk of Cuenca regarded him as a saint. Father Crespi died in 1982 and the people built a monument in his name that is, to this day, decorated every day with fresh flowers. What was so special about this padre? He listened to the Indios—for hours, or even days if need be. He won their trust and helped them out in all sorts of difficult situations.

The Indios expressed their gratitude by showering gifts upon the kindly preacher. The religious artifacts are of the kind that aren't exactly approved of by the Catholic Church; artifacts that their families had kept hidden from the white men for hundreds of years. Father Crespi initially placed the objects against the wall of his inner courtyard. But as their number increased, he was forced to start piling them up in a shed behind the church. The flow of gifts, however, didn't let up, and Crespi was forced to open up two further rooms in which he piled up some of the most amazing treasures that I have ever seen.

More items from Father Crespi's collection.

Some of the artifacts in the Crespi collection are elaborately carved.

Panels, figures, and totems stacked up against each other.

Scientists have never really thoroughly examined Father Crespi's treasures. It has even been claimed that they were all modern fakes and forgeries. Well, it is quite possible that some of the panels, figures, and totems were indeed made in the last century, but some of them can't possibly have been. Since the arrival of the Spanish conquistadores, the indigenous peoples of South America have been devout Christians, yet there is no trace of Christian imagery on any of the pieces in Crespi's collection: no cross, no Madonna, no Jesus, no biblical quotes. The artistic style of the artifacts originates from a pre-Christian epoch. The faces on the metal panels are outlandish, and the entire style and countless symbols do not fit in with any customary art-historical thinking. Often, the engraved metal panels are so complex and so extensively complemented by innumerable small illustrations that one is tempted to think of them as belonging to a unique school.

There are metal panels lying around with serial narratives, and no one pays them the slightest bit of attention. There is a confusing cornucopia of images that make up compositions that flow into one another. Faces with solar coronas and heads reminiscent of giraffes with radiating beams, intertwined with apelike, anxious-looking faces with snakes growing out of them. All in all, there are too many details for them to be simple forgeries, and too much background knowledge for a single mad genius. One of the golden panels features stars in its upper left- and right-hand corners, then a being with a bloated belly and snakelike tail, a ratlike creature, a man in an armored tunic with attached helmet, a triangular figure with a hole through its middle, and—on the opposite side—a figure with rays shooting out of his head.

Finally, there are faces, wheels, birds, snakes, and—in the middle—something that looks like an arrow pointing downward. It's chaos at a level to match the Voynich manuscript, but not a good candidate for a forgery because there's nothing there that could really be forged or copied. But this is just the beginning, and maybe we are starting to get a little closer to solving the Voynich riddle.

A stone pyramid featuring undecipherable writing and an elephant.

Father Crespi was not just some adventurous figure who popped up out of the blue. He was a priest, and the Indios told him that their treasures all came from the secret stores of their forefathers. What reason could the Indios have had to lie to their so well-respected and loved padre? Or to present him with cheap, homemade kitsch? I'm really grateful that I had the chance to take pictures of this unique collection while Father Crespi was still alive.

It is possible—on the other hand—to argue about the material these incomparable art works are made of. Crespi himself believed that below the golden surface of these metal panels one would actually find pure gold. But you need to know that the even the pre-Inca tribes had mastered unbelievably complex techniques for smelting and making alloys that we are unable to duplicate even today.[20] Their sophisticated casting techniques and gilding processes used a mixture of 50-percent copper, 25-percent silver, and 25-percent gold. The external color of an object has little reflection of the amount of gold actually used. The Incas were able coat objects with a gold layer that was only half a micrometer thick and—when viewed through a microscope—only visible at a magnification level of 500×. They had mastered techniques that allowed them to give any base metal the appearance of pure gold.

When an alloy of copper-silver-tin or even copper-gold-tin is heated, the noble metal enhances the surface of the metal while the copper component is gradually lost to oxidation. Finally, the surface gsins the appearance of pure gold. If the alloy contains both silver and gold, both metals come to the surface, giving the metal a pale silvery or pale yellow sheen. It seems as if the unknown artists intentionally plated their messages with a thin coating of precious metal so that they would survive the millennia. Just like the Voynich manuscript, the Crespi collection defies categorization.

"Stylized spermatozoa, grinning suns, the crescent of a waning moon."

Amazing and Impossible

Thirty-five years ago, I photographed some amazing and impossible things in Carlo Crespi's storerooms. There was a disc with a diameter of around 22 centimeters decorated with stylized spermatozoa, grinning suns, the crescent of a waning moon, a large star, and two square, manlike faces.

I also saw a pyramid, flanked on the left and right by jumping cats. In the sky was a snake, above the pyramid a sun, and on each side of that four and five squiggles. Along the base of the pyramid is an unmistakable band of rune-like characters—symbols that no one has ever been able to decipher—and on each side of the pyramid's base, an elephant. Heaven help us! There have never been elephants roaming around South America, neither before nor after the Incas. Admittedly, elephant bones have been excavated in Mexico, but they are said to be more than 12,000 years old. I also found a similar set of symbols—16 of them, arranged in a four-by-four square—decorating a gilded collar. The pictures prove it.

The craziest piece that Crespi showed me, however—and, according to the man himself, it came from an underground metal library, about which I'll tell you more in the next chapter—was a gilded metal panel with 56 squares. The panel is divided into 14 horizontal strips, each strip into four squares, and each square depicting a character that appeared to have been stamped into the metal. Some of these symbols display an uncanny similarity to symbols from the Voynich manuscript. Could this panel be some kind of Rosetta Stone for decrypting the Voynich manuscript? I know no more than you, my dear reader, but one thing I can tell you—and indeed with some certainty—and that is that thousands of years ago there were texts that were never registered in any library and that were brought to the Earth by extraterrestrial beings. Texts that defy any earthly logic, that contradict the symmetry of every alphabet, and that could only ever be translated when enough material was available for comparison. Texts by aliens? A little far-fetched? When are they supposed to have been here? How? What technology did the ETs use to span the light years and, even then, what on Earth could they want from us? And to top it all, they left us texts? A pretty crazy notion! How can we corroborate this? Well, there really are historical writings that back up the idea of extraterrestrial texts—it's just that no one knows about them. Here is the dossier:

An Intergalactic Dossier?

In his dialog *Phaedrus,* the philosopher Plato quotes a history that he heard from Socrates:[21]

"At the Egyptian city of Naucratis, there was a famous old god, whose name was Theuth; the bird which is called the Ibis is sacred to him, and he was the inventor of many arts, such as arithmetic and calculation and geometry and astronomy and draughts and dice, but his great discovery was the use of letters...."

The god Theuth passed on the gift of writing to the pharaoh:

"This, said Theuth, will make the Egyptians wiser and give them better memories; it is a specific both for the memory and for the wit."

The pharaoh saw another side to this marvelous invention and contradicted the god Theuth:

"...this discovery of yours will create forgetfulness in the learners' souls, because they will not use their memories; they will trust to the external written characters and not remember of themselves. The specific which you have discovered is an aid not to memory, but to reminiscence...."

And indeed, he was right: these millennia-old texts can only recall events that are otherwise long forgotten. Who remembers, for example, that God—whoever he, she, or it may be—created other worlds long before the creation of Earth? It can be read in the ancient legends of the Jews:

Thousands of worlds did the Lord create in the beginning; then he created still more worlds.... The Lord created worlds and then destroyed them; he planted trees and pulled them up again, for they were still confused...and he continued to create worlds and to destroy worlds until he created our world. Then he spake: This world is a great pleasure to me, those others pleased me not.[22]

Creating and destroying worlds because they didn't quite fit the bill? In today's parlance, we call that "terraforming."[23] That is a process for transforming uninhabitable planets into worlds that are fit for human habitation. One such idea involves dumping large quantities of cyanobacteria into the Martian atmosphere. These bacteria multiply rapidly and, in the process, produce large quantities of oxygen.

Was it really mankind that—during a long and drawn out process of becoming intelligent—thought up the idea of writing down symbols to preserve knowledge? *Of course! Who else?* I hear you cry. Can you be so sure? The ancient legends tell that writing existed two thousand years before the creation of "intelligent" man. Back then, there were no scrolls of parchment and no animals whose skins could be used, not even metal. And in the absence of trees, no wooden panels, this book existed in the form of a hallowed sapphire. An angel named Raziel, "the very same one who sat by the stream that flowed out of Eden," passed this strange "book" on to our progenitor, Adam.[24] It must have been a wholly curious specimen, because it contained not only all that was worth knowing, but also prophecies about the future. Adam was to draw wealth from this wonderful book and all those who came after him: "Also, of your children who will come after you...will any who use this book...know what is to come. Whether it be misfortune, the coming of hunger, whether the grain will be too plentiful or too scarce, whether deluge or drought will reign in the land."[25]

How can any lexicon or even encyclopedia today compare to that kind of superbook? We need to seek the authors of that phenomenal work among the heavenly legions, for after the angel Raziel had given our ancestor the book and even read a little from it for him, something quite amazing followed:

"And in that hour, when Adam received the book, arose a great flame on the banks of the river, and the angel rode up in the blaze into heaven."[26]

Angels or ETs?

While we're on the subject: what *is* an angel exactly? They appear in practically every piece of religious literature, and they are definitely not of this Earth. And they are clearly not spirits that could be dreamt up or imagined, for these angels are in the possession of some pretty powerful weapons, which they use to chastise mankind. Some of them even had their wicked way with the daughters of men (I'll be getting back to that later in "The Truth Behind Enoch" section)—which isn't exactly a fine or heavenly manner of behaving. So if angels were not terrestrial, the only option that remains is that they were extraterrestrial. And these angels (extraterrestrials) knew about the future?

It's simple, really. When man is finally capable of interstellar spaceflight and lands on a planet peopled by Stone Age beings, we probably won't find it too hard to tell these natives a thing or two about their futures either.

Of course, I don't mean predictions about individuals, but rather about their future societies. We could tell them about specific technologies that they will invent, because they are an intrinsic part of development, or how they will suffer from environmental problems if their population grows without check—because you can't have one without the other. Or, even better: we will prophesize about how their descendents will be able to split the tiniest units of matter; how this will be dangerous because it could lead to the destruction of great swathes of the planet, making them uninhabitable for centuries (H-bombs). This trick can also be used for smaller periods of time, such as future harvests, plagues of locusts, or the seeming immortality of the cockchafer. The indigenous people might not understand any of it, but they can write it down and preserve the knowledge for the future.

A Magical Book

In the story of Adam's book, it's the same thing:

Within the book were embedded the higher symbols of the holy wisdom, and the seventy-two types of sciences were contained therein, which in their place were divided into the six hundred and seventy symbols of the higher secrets. Also, the fifteen hundred keys, which were not entrusted to the holy ones of the upper world, were hidden in that book.[27]

Did you know that there were "seventy-two types of sciences" that can be further subdivided into "six hundred and seventy symbols" of even higher knowledge? It's a bit like our subdivision of physics into atomic physics, particle physics, astrophysics, and so on. Or the umbrella term *biology,* which covers a spectrum from single-celled animals, to insects, elephants, and right on up to exobiology.

Adam bequeathed this magical book to his 10-year-old son Seth. He must have been a pretty switched-on lad, because Adam told him in detail "about the strengths of the book," but also "wherein its power and miracles lie."[28] He also explained to him how he had used the book and that he had hidden it in a cleft in a rock.

Seth received the paternal instructions, learned diligently from the holy sapphire, and finally constructed "...a golden ark, laid the book within and hid the ark in a cave...."[29]

Much later, the knowledge from the sapphire passed into the hands of Noah, the man who saved mankind from the Flood, and he used it to understand the courses of the planets through the heavens, "also the paths of Aldebaran, Orion and Sirius...also the names of every individual heaven...and the names of the heavenly servants."[30]

The fantastic story of the Adam book could quite easily be filed away under "just a story," if it weren't for a few things that just go against the grain.

I understand the urge to slip a book—metaphorically speaking—to our ancient ancestor, because the lonesome patriarch must have gotten his knowledge from somewhere. But the idea with the sapphire I find harder to swallow. How on Earth did they come up with that one? The concept of an encyclopedia stored on a precious jewel would have been pretty obscure for a few centuries ago, let alone a few millennia. These days, we have technologies that allow us to store copious quantities of data onto crystals. And Adam is said to have carried on dialogs with this book. How did that come about? Where did the author of this story get that idea from? Nowadays, just about everyone has "dialogs" with his or her computer. But that kind of thinking just doesn't fit in with the ancient past. And where did the idea come from, all those thousands of years ago, to add details to the Adam story such as the "seventy-two types of sciences," which the book is said to contain? Or the "six hundred and seventy symbols of the higher secrets" and the "fifteen hundred keys"? Specific information like that doesn't just come off the cuff. I don't want to overrate the contents of this long-lost book, and yet I have to ask myself why the storyteller placed such value on specific constellations of stars. Why was it important to Adam or his descendents to know the astronomical paths of Aldebaran, Sirius, or Orion? They're not of any use for any terrestrial calendar.

Adam, Seth, and Noah are also said to have learned the names of the individual heavens from this book, too. Wait a minute! Isn't there just one heaven? What are they talking about?

In fact, we can learn about them in the ancient Jewish legends.[31] The first heaven is called *Wilon,* from which all mankind is observed. Above Wilon lies *Raqia,* wherein the stars and planets lie. The next level is called *Shehaqim,* and above lie *Zebul, Maon,* and *Makon.* Finally, above Makon, lies the seventh and highest heaven, called *Araboth.* This is said to be the home of the *Cherubim* and some kind of heavenly bodies known as *Holy Wheels.* Often, the distances between the different heavens are also provided, along with units of measurement and time periods: between the heavens, for instance, lie "ladders" and "epochs spanning five hundred years." It all sounds an awful lot like space travel.

This pepped-up tale from ancient time sounds thoroughly implausible. Nothing more than "foolish fantasy," as the theologian Dr. Eisenmenger mockingly claimed almost three hundred years ago.[32] Legends are an imprecise form of story-telling: grotesque and wonderful, fascinating and bloodcurdling at the same time. What's more, legends tend to pay little attention to chronology and are not worried in the slightest about historical facts. The legend is "popular speculation and popular fantasy"[33] and yet remains in the popular memory. Legends and myths, however, are not built on nothing. They are not simply tall stories; they always contain a kernel of truth that quite often also crops up—presto!—in the traditions of numerous other peoples or civilizations, albeit with other names and other heroes.

A Creature From the Sea

I'm no closer to the Voynich manuscript than before. But I wanted to concentrate on my theory that gods or angels—in other words, beings that are not of this Earth—had dictated or otherwise passed on books to mankind. Maybe you've heard of the legendary creature *Oannes* (Sumerian: Abgallu)?

At a time when Alexander the Great still reigned over Babylon (around 350 B.C.), there lived a priest and historian of Marduk (also known as Bel or Ba'al) called Berossus. Berossus wrote a three-volume work in the Greek language, the *Babyloniaca.* The first book dealt with astronomy and the creation of the world; the second dealt with the 10 kings that reigned before the flood and the 86 kings that followed; the third book is a history chronicling the period up to the time of Alexander the Great. Unfortunately only fragments of the *Babyloniaca* remain, but Lucius Seneca and Flavius Josephus, a contemporary of Jesus, quote from it. Berossus refers to a much older document, writing:

In the first year there appeared, from that part of the Erythræan Sea [today's Persian Gulf], which borders upon Babylonia, an animal endowed with reason, by the name of Oannes.... Its voice was articulate and human, and an image of him has been preserved to this day. This creature spent its days among men, but ate no food; and gave them insights into letters and sciences, and arts of every kind. He taught them to build cities and temples, how to draw up laws and measure the land. He showed them how to sow the seeds and how to collect the fruits; he instructed them in everything which could humanize their lives. From that time, nothing material has been added by way of improvement to his instructions. *Oannes also wrote a book about the genesis of man and the origin of civil states, which he then gave to mankind* [author's italics].[34]

Does this book even exist anywhere? Is there, perhaps, a copy hidden somewhere beneath an ancient temple, watched over by cowled guardians who themselves have no idea what kind of treasure is in their hands? It seems clear that Oannes's book of learning, even in Berossus's time, wasn't simply to be found in the nearest library. So, is it all just chitchat?

Wait a moment! In the holy book of the Parsees, the *Avesta,* a mysterious being named *Yma* appears from the sea and instructs the people. In the legends of the Phoenicians a creature with the same origins and abilities was known as *Taut,* and in ancient China, at the time of Emperor *Fuk-Hi,* a creature called *Meng-ho* arose from the water: "a monster with the body of a horse and the head of a dragon, whose back was laden with tablets filled with letters."[35] The great Tibetan master *Padmasambhava* (also known as *U-Rgyab Pad-Ma*) brought down incomprehensible texts from the heavens. Before he died, his students deposited these texts in a cave for later times, "*in which they could be understood*" [author's italics].[36] Most probably, we would have just as much luck deciphering them as we've had with the Voynich manuscript—and that was only written a few hundred years ago!

Wisdom From the Gods

And where did mankind even get all these methods of writing from? Are they all simply made up? Cuneiform, hieroglyphics, alphabets? If you believe the ancient chroniclers, it was those self-same ominous gods who taught their respective "chosen ones" how to write. They probably sought out the most intelligent people they could find.

Diodorus of Sicily, the author of a 40-volume historical library, tells in his first book how the gods founded many cities in Egypt alone and also how they had left their progeny behind them: "First the gods weaned mankind from cannibalism."[37] Then they taught man—according to Diodorus—the arts, mining, how to make tools, how to till the soil and how to make wine. Even the art of writing came from the gods: "Namely, it was they who first categorized and developed all the comprehensible languages, and much was given a name for which previously there had been no concept. The invention of writing also was down to him [the god]...."[38]

These stories clearly originate from more than just one single ancient source. The fragments all fit, just like in a crime novel. And you don't have to be Sherlock Holmes to put all the individual pieces together. These gods and angels existed—even if the thought of it makes us want to tear our hair out. And they wrought changes, too. The greatest witness to all this was Enoch, and writing about him again is almost embarrassing, as I've already dealt with him in numerous books. But to stress my assertion that it was some kind of extraterrestrial figures—call them gods or angels if you will—who instructed mankind, gave them letters, and even taught them how to write, it's pretty hard to ignore Enoch. He is namely the only eyewitness who experienced everything in person and wrote all of his chronicles in the first person, the "I" form. Enoch is a perfect example of how twisted theology has, for many centuries, managed to falsify the truth and sweep the facts under the carpet, and to turn a work based on personal experience into a hocus pocus of gibberish and interpretation—and it really makes me pretty angry just think-ing about it. Yet it is not really all that difficult to debunk some of these theological irritations. You just need to examine the content.

With Enoch, of course, I am faced with the same dilemma as in each previous book: how do I explain something to my readers without constantly repeating things I have written before? Schoolteachers and university lectur-ers have an easier time of it. They can assume that their students already understand the basics. If you don't know your ABCs, you can't read. But I can't assume that you already know about Enoch. Maybe you are a new reader, one who has just discovered my way of looking at things. And on top of that, many of my older books are no longer in print. So, what can I do? I'll try and cut this Gordian knot by restricting myself to repeating only what is necessary for the new reader, whereby the repetitions will not exactly be repetitions. A note to my faithful long-term readers: you will find out things about Enoch in this book that have never been revealed before.

Although I'm no fan of convoluted theological literature, I admire the men who are responsible for creating it (and yes, we are just speaking about men here!). The translators of the ancient Enoch texts were all extremely well educated. Without exception, they spoke many languages, were men of integrity, and made a sincere effort to unravel the millennia-old confusion. But they were all theologians, which derives from the words *theos* (god) and *logos* (word)—the word of God. But that's not precisely what theology deals with. All these theologians of bygone days were, of course, thoroughly con-vinced that they were working on the words of God—otherwise they may never have chosen that career—but this very conviction is already an aspect of faith. They truly believed that these holy, and sometimes not-so-holy, writ-ings came directly from the mouth of God, that he had dictated them or revealed them in some wonderful way to the chosen. What remains of texts when the element of belief is removed? The words themselves. They have lost nothing except their sanctity. They may remain venerable, because they are old; one may treat them with respect, because they reveal events from ages that are lost to us; and they should be scientifically analyzed, because they are packed with extremely interesting material. As soon as a text has lost its sanctity, it can be discussed objectively. It is our conception of the inviolability of these texts that prevents any topical analysis.

So, let's start to really stir up some trouble!

The Story of Enoch

Who is this Enoch character?

In "The Ancient Legends of the Jews," Enoch is a "king over all men," who reigned for exactly 243 years. In the book of Genesis, Enoch is mentioned as one of the ten patriarchs who ruled before the flood. In the Bible, Enoch is dealt with in five sentences (Genesis 5:21-24): "(21) When Enoch had lived 65 years, he became the father of Methuselah. (22) And after he became the father of Methuselah, Enoch walked with God 300 years and had other sons and daughters. (23) Altogether, Enoch lived 365 years. (24) Enoch walked with God; then he was no more, because God took him away."[38]

Just like that—gone in the blink of an eye. In the Hebrew language the word *Enoch* means "the initiated one," "the insightful one," or "the skillful one." And this initiated one made sure, God be praised, that his knowledge didn't disappear with him, much to the chagrin of those fools who would rather have seen Enoch and all his knowledge go up in smoke. Because Enoch is dynamite for today's society—and that's where the trouble starts. But let's take a step back: what do other peoples, apart from the Israelites, have to say about Enoch?

In ancient Egypt, Enoch was the builder of the Great Pyramid, or at least that is the claim made by Taqi al-Din Ahmad ibn Ali ibn Abd al-Qadir ibn Muhammad al-Maqrizi (1363-1442) in his work *Khitat.* He noted that Enoch was known by different names among the different peoples: *Saurid, Hermes, Idris,* and *Enoch.* Here is the passage from the *Khitat,* chapter 33:

...the first Hermes, who was named thrice in his capacity as prophet, king and wise man (it is he who Hebrews name Enoch, son of Jared, son of Mahalel, son of Kenan, son of Enos, son of Seth, son of Adam—praised be his name—and that is Idris), he read in the stars that the flood would come. Then he had the pyramids built and *hid within them treasures, learned books* and everything which he feared could be otherwise lost, so that those things would remain safe [author's italics].[40]

According to the Sumerian king list "WB444," an engraved stone block that can be admired in the British Museum in London, 10 great kings ruled between the creation and the flood. The entire length of their reigns was 456,000 years. After the flood, the kingship descended once more from heaven, according to the Sumerian king list. It seemed as though they had liked it on the blue planet. The 23 kings that occupied the throne after the flood managed a lesser, but still not insignificant total of 24,510 years, three months, and three and a half days in charge. The seventh of the antediluvian rulers is said to have lived in the city of sun, *Sippar.* The gods Shamash and Adad are said to have selected him to be the first to learn the arts of writing and prophecy. This seventh king, according to the Bible, would have been Enoch. The fame of this seventh king was so great that in later years the great Babylonian ruler Nebuchadnezzar I (around 1100 B.C.) was said to have derived his bloodline from him. Translations of cuneiform writings made over the last few decades have revealed that it was precisely this seventh king "who ascended into heaven."[41] Like Enoch. Sumerologists, like theologians, both of whom swim in the currents of contemporary rationality, interpret this as some kind of "rapture" and thus describe the cuneiform texts as the "earliest written record of an ascension."[42] The figure of this seventh ruler of the sun city Sippar "inspired the religious fantasy and fabulizing of later Judaism."[43] The proof of this is the coalescence of various fragments from the diverse Enoch books. But now I will show you why this notion is somewhat wide of the mark.

The Discovery of the Book of Enoch

The news that the Book of Enoch had been found reached Europe in the first half of the 18th century. While exploring Africa, Scottish adventurer James Bruce (1730-1794) not only discovered the source of the Blue Nile, he also brought three copies of an Enoch text back with him to London. The texts were translated into somewhat poor English by Professor Richard Laurence, but Enoch didn't really become a subject of scientific discussion until German orientalist and protestant theologian August Dillman (1823-1894) translated the scrolls into German. Since then, more than 30 more Ethiopian manuscripts have been added to the original documents. But where did Bruce get his hands on the texts?

When the church fathers edited—or, to use the technical term, canonized—the Bible in the fourth century, they had many more texts than now appear in the Bible. But many of these texts were incomplete, had gaps in them or were just plain incomprehensible. So these fragments didn't make it into the Bible. Nevertheless, these rejected texts were not simply thrown out; instead, they were put to one side—including Enoch texts. The texts later came to be referred to as the "Apocrypha and Pseudoepigrapha of the Old Testament."[44] The Abyssinian church, on the other hand, had adopted Enoch into its canon—one good reason why James Bruce found the text in Ethiopia. Later on, a Slavonic variant of the same Book of Enoch also turned up, and highly academic textual comparisons revealed that the similarities of the fundamental aspects of the two books could only be attributed to common authorship. And that's where the theological arguments started.

The Book of Enoch describes many impossible things: journeys into the heavens, visits to other worlds, astronomical teachings, conversations with "angels" and a being with the appellation "Most High," and tribunals for "fallen angels" and men. What does it all mean?

Theologians and classical scholars, men with phenomenal linguistic ability, yet all following their "theos logos" and religious psychology, all looked for solutions. What else could they have done? Enoch's descriptions are turned into "parables" (sometimes called "similitudes"), "visions," "inspirations," "dreams," "inventions," "stories," or—and this really takes the biscuit—it is claimed that the entire Book of Enoch is the work of several Jewish priests and the whole thing is simply a "personification of the Jewish race."[45]

And indeed, the Book of Enoch has been repeatedly doctored and changed around—much like the urtexts of the New Testament. For instance, the term *son of man* crops up and it can be seen that it has been added later in an Ethiopian hand. Similarly, the terms *the chosen* and *the just.* Theologians argue that these terms refer to the Jewish race. The whole thing became even more confusing when, sometime in the fifth century, a Hebrew version of the Book of Enoch featuring countless elaborations also did the rounds, but was not taken seriously because it was—allegedly—based on a vision experienced by the Jewish *Rabbi Ishma'el.* That led to the Book of Enoch being lumped together with the *Gnostic writings.* Today, Gnosticism is generally associated with a kind of esoteric philosophy, weltanschauung, or religion. The word *gnosis* is Greek and means "recognition."

Regardless of where *Rabbi Ishma'el* got his mysterious information from, he could not possibly have simply made it up, because it is far too complicated and detailed. Before I march on to the Slavonic and Greek versions of the Book of Enoch, here are a few highly curious snippets of information from the Hebrew text.

The Hebrew Book of Enoch

Rabbi Ishma'el claims to have traveled up to heaven and met with an angel called *Metatron,* who then showed him around. This same Metatron then revealed himself to be none other than Enoch. Unlike the other versions, in the Hebrew book Metatron/Enoch is not able to return to Earth and to mankind, but instead remains in the vicinity of the throne of the "Most High" and only the seer Rabbi Ishma'el can reach him. Metatron/Enoch tells the Rabbi that the Lord calls him "Youth." He explains why: "Happy art thou and happy is thy father for thy Creator doth favor thee. And because I am small and a youth among them in days, months and years, therefore they call me 'Youth.'"[46]

And how did Metatron/Enoch come to be in the heavenly realm?

When the Holy One, blessed be He, desired to lift me up on high, He first sent *Anaphiel,* the prince, and he took me from their midst before their very eyes and carried me in great glory upon a fiery chariot drawn by fiery horses.... When the Holy One, blessed be He, took me away from the generation of the Flood, he lifted me on the wings of the wind of *Shekina* to the highest heaven and brought me into the great palaces of the *Araboth Raqia* on high, where [can be seen] the glorious Throne of *Shekina.*[47]

We find out that "Holy One" loves the Youth (Metatron/Enoch) very much; indeed he loves him even "more than all [his] servants" and has thus written letters with a flaming stylus and revealed to Metatron/Enoch not only how Heaven and Earth came into being, but also the seas and rivers, mountains and hills, lightning, thunder, sound and storm, and even the planets and constellations.

Not bad, this all-embracing, interstellar knowledge given to Metatron/ Enoch. A thought at the back of my mind brings me to Abraham, who also ascended into Heaven and saw the Earth "under him."[48] Or *Enkidu* from the Epic of Gilgamesh, who is carried out across the Earth on "eagle's wings."[49,50] Or "Arjuna's journey to Indra's heaven."[51] And when heavenly "Wheels" or "halls in the firmament" appear in the Hebrew Book of Enoch, I am reminded of the "wheels" in the *Book of Dzyan*[52] and the "heavenly cities" in the Sanskrit epic *Mahabharata.*[53] There are countless similar cases scattered throughout classical literature. The difference between the theologians and myself is that I look at texts from all religions and regions of the world, while the scholars of the Judaeo-Christian tradition restrict themselves exclusively to the writings in the Bible and the Apocrypha. Every single one of them.

In the Hebrew Book of Enoch, *Rabbi Ishma'el* lists a plethora of different worlds (planets) along with their denominations. He knows the names of each of their leaders, princes, or kings, and even tells of a *heavenly library*: "He brought forth the casket of writings with the Book of Memories and placed them before the Holy One, praised be He. And he broke open the seal of the casket, opened it, took the books from within and gave them to the Holy One, praised be He...."[54]

Heaven, saints, Most High, princes, servants, archangels, wheels, planets, fiery chariots, heavenly legions—heaven help us! Did this Enoch even exist? So far, I have told you seven of his aliases: *Enoch, Saurid, Hermes, Idris, Metatron, "Youth,"* and the *seventh antediluvian king.* Which is the right one, then?

Probably none of our phonetic spellings or pronunciations. Biblical Hebrew was a language written purely in consonants—no vowels at all. To make it easier to read, the vowels are indicated, if at all, by a system of dots (niqqud). A phonetic-reading of Enoch could therefore just as easily be Inich, Onuch, or Anich, and Metatron could even be Mototran. Here, of course, I am not taking the cabbalistic interpretations into account, because in that system each letter can even also be assigned a numerical value.

Hebrew experts estimate that the Ethiopian texts were originally written between the fifth and second centuries B.C.—and that leads us to the first problem. From the texts themselves, it emerges that the texts deal with the history of the seventh patriarch. His name was—we'll stick with the standard form—Enoch. Therefore, his name was appended to the Books of Enoch. Enoch, for his part, did not live, however, between the fifth and second centuries B.C.

That means that the original content must have been written down much earlier, before the flood. This is confirmed by the author himself, as you can clearly see from the following examples:[55] (The numbers in parentheses refer to chapter and verse.)

(81, 1 ff) "And he said unto me: 'Observe, Enoch, these heavenly tablets, read what is written thereon, and mark you well every single fact.' And I observed the heavenly tablets, and read everything which was written thereon...."

(82, 1) "And now, my son Methuselah, all these things I am recounting to thee and writing down for thee! ...preserve, my son Methuselah, the books thou hast received from thy father's hand, and deliver them to the generations of the world...."

(83, 2) "Two visions I saw before I took a wife, and the one was quite unlike the other: the first when I was learning to write: the second before I took thy mother...."

(87, 3 ff) "And those three that had last come forth grasped me by my hand and took me up, away from the generations of the earth, and raised me up to a lofty place, and showed me a tower raised high above the earth, and all the hills were lower."

(91, 1) "And now, my son Methuselah, call to me all thy brothers and gather together to me all the sons of thy mother...."

(92, 1) "Enoch indeed wrote this complete doctrine of wisdom...."

These quotes show that it was Enoch, however he might have been known during his own lifetime, who wrote the verses. He confirms his authorship by his use of the first person, as if he had feared that the minds of the future might otherwise have been too limited to understand. And indeed, to this very day exegetes ignore the fact that this document is written in the first person. The original of the book, its essence, comes from the antediluvian Enoch, otherwise he could hardly have spoken of Methuselah as his son, or have listed his lineage back to Adam. To claim that it is some kind of pre-Christian forgery is to accuse the author of lying from start to finish. To deny that Enoch is the antediluvian author is to cast the whole of exegesis into a poor light and is also a fundamental departure from reality. It's yet another outrageous example of how the faithful have been manipulated. Of course, the Book of Enoch is passed off as a "vision." It's a standard method of putting aside just about anything that is otherwise hard to swallow. The fact that Enoch repeatedly says that he is fully awake is swept under the carpet. And in addition to that, he gives his family explicit instructions of what to do after his departure. It can hardly have been a "vision of his own death"—another bright idea from the exegetes—as the highly literate Enoch returned from his meeting with the angels fit as a fiddle. Only at the end of the story does he take his final leave of his kinsmen—in a chariot of fire.

The Truth Behind Enoch

Enoch, or Mister X—I think I'll stick with the seventh patriarch and call him Enoch from now on—lived in an age that understood nothing of modern technology. There is no way he could have known about mother ships, shuttle craft, headlamps, loudspeakers, radio devices, booming motors, and so on. Everything that he experienced had to be paraphrased so that he was even in a position to describe it, because he simply didn't have the vocabulary. Just *you* try, dear reader, to describe a helicopter or a radio to a Stone Age man. You inevitably end up in some kind of "it-looks-like-this" game. Or try explaining a spiral staircase to somebody without using any pictures. You'll need to use your hands—at the very least!

And this mess gets even worse with every new generation that attempts to understand and interpret the Enoch text and—of course!—completely fails to understand what is being described. Incapable of understanding that what they read, later scribes delved into the fantasy of their oriental metaphors and thus arose opulent allegorical stories. Later, as the theologians of the last 200 years began to interpret the texts from a religious perspective, the chaos was finally perfect. Finally, perfectly ordinary space travelers became angels and cherubim, officers became archangels, and the supreme commander became the "Most High" or, even worse, God. What pandemonium, when a simple electrical discharge is transformed into "a tongue of fire," and the command bridge becomes "the indescribable glory." It's understandable that, from a theological point of view, the captain's chair of command is transformed into a mighty throne and the incomprehensible mishmash of similitudes is turned into stories and visions.

I have never heard a convincing counterargument, despite all the fabulous discussions I have had with Old Testament experts, and the absolute torrent of theological literature that I have tried to digest. My interpretations of the text must be false: maybe I should look at it from another angle. But why? After all, alternative explanations—not least those that have arisen from exegesis—have only yielded nonsense and the core statements in the text are reflected in so many texts from outside of the Judaeo-Christian tradition.

The first five chapters of the Book of Enoch announce (allegedly) some kind of Last Judgment: the God of Heaven will leave his abode and descend to Earth with his legions of Angels. The following eleven chapters describe what happens to the so-called "apostate angels" who—in direct contravention to God's commandments—"defiled" themselves with the daughters of men. These "angels" were given tasks by their "God" that were so precise that they just don't fit in with the cohorts of the heavenly host. For example:

"Semjaza taught enchantments, and root cuttings, Armaros the resolving of enchantments, Baraqijal taught astrology, Kokabel the constellations, Ezeqeel the knowledge of the clouds, Araqiel the signs of the earth, Shamsiel the signs of the sun, and Sariel the course of the moon...."[56]

This is a range of specialized subjects that were way beyond the ken of earthly dwellers at that time.

Chapters 17–36 describe Enoch's journeys to the various worlds and distant spheres. Theologians call these similitudes or parables, or Enoch's journey to the magical garden (The Garden of Righteousness). Yet Enoch was ordered to write down these so-called "similitudes" to preserve them for future generations. What was the reason for this? Simple: his contemporaries were just not capable of understanding these messages; they were *intended* for future folk. And that's not my interpretation; that's from the book itself!

Chapters 72-82 are known as the "astronomy chapters." This is where Enoch receives instruction about the orbits of the sun and the moon, about leap years, about the stars and celestial mechanics. The remaining chapters contain conversations with his son Methuselah, in which he announces the coming flood. The whole thing is crowned by Enoch's departure in a flaming chariot—what else?

The Slavonic Book of Enoch contains interesting details that are not to be found in such detail in the Abyssinian version:

> After this too I lived two hundred years and completed of all the years of my life three hundred and sixty five years. On the first day of the first month I was in my house alone...there appeared to me two men of enormous size, the like of which I never saw on earth. Their faces were like the sun, their eyes too were like a burning light, and from their lips came coming fire; their clothing and song were splendid; their wings were brighter than gold, their hands whiter than snow. They were standing at the head of my couch and called me by my name. I arose from my sleep and saw clearly those two men standing in front of me. I saluted them and was seized with fear and the appearance of my face was changed from terror, and those men said to me: "Have courage, Enoch, do not fear; the eternal God sent us to thee, and lo! today thou shalt ascend with us into heaven, and thou shalt tell thy sons and all thy household all that they shall do without thee on earth in thy house, and let no one seek thee till the Lord return thee to them."[57]

The theological interpretation that the antediluvian patriarch is experiencing a vision or a dream here is not tenable. Enoch awakes, gets up from his bed, and then proceeds to give his kinsfolk instructions as to what they are to do in his absence. The "death vision" variation also makes no sense, as Enoch returns to his family after his trip to outer space. So, what did he experience "up there"?

Enoch Learns the Secrets of the Universe

Enoch learned to write, and books were dictated to him. Not, of course, that God himself dictated the knowledge personally. This was carried out by an archangel called Pravuil. And to make sure everything ran quickly and smoothly, Pravuil gave Enoch "a reed of quick-writing":

> And the Lord summoned one of his archangels by the name of Pravuil, whose knowledge was quicker in wisdom than the other archangels, who wrote all the deeds of the Lord; and the Lord said to Pravuil: "Bring out the books from my storehouses, *and take a reed of quick-writing, and give it to Enoch, and deliver to him the choice and comforting books out of thy hand....*"[58] [author's italics]

What was this important wisdom that had to be dictated? Actually, everything, because mankind down below knew very little. Enoch continued: "And it was told me all the works of heaven, earth and sea, and all the elements their passages and goings, and the thunderings of the thunders, the sun and moon, the goings and changes of the stars, the seasons, years, days, and hours, the risings of the wind...and for thirty days and thirty nights he spake, never stopping."[59]

And, as if that wasn't enough, the first marathon sitting was followed by another, equally long dictation. Enoch was truly a model student.

Whenever the conversation turns to Enoch and I suggest that the antediluvian prophet was privileged to have taken a course in a spaceship crewed by extraterrestrials, I always hear, *Well, he must have had some sort of spacesuit.* Must he? More likely, the aliens would have had to protect themselves against bacteria and viruses and probably even human perspiration. What does the attentive student Enoch have to say?

> And the Lord said to Michael: "Go and take Enoch from out his earthly garments, and anoint him with my sweet ointment, and put him into the garments of My glory." And Michael did thus, as the Lord told him. He anointed me, and dressed me, and the appearance of that ointment is more than the great light, and his ointment is like sweet dew, and its smell as myrrh, shining like the sun's rays, and I looked at myself, and was like one of his glorious ones.[60]

Now try to imagine that this entire description has got something to do with the "dear Lord" of the Christian religion. He had a special salve and gave the order to rub down Enoch with this intensely aromatic paste? We humans always had peculiar tastes! And then, Enoch was unclothed and then redressed in some kind of outfit that left him looking just like all the others. Of course! In a spacesuit, or at least a uniform: what else? And after finally being brought to the bridge, or perhaps some sort of conference room—or, as the theologians see it, before the "throne of the Great Glory"—Enoch told how the majestic leader arose and "came to me and spoke to me with his voice."[61]

Here, at the very latest is where it gets embarrassing for the exegetes. It's not really a scene that you can ascribe to God. Two extraterrestrials ("the like of which I never saw on earth") collected Enoch, disinfected him, dressed him in a spacesuit, and brought him to the command bridge of the mother ship, and God welcomed him "with his voice." He then gave instructions that Enoch was to be giving a "reed of quick-writing" and then a subaltern named *Pravuil* was given the task of dictating scientific books to him for days on end. Is it any great surprise that the interpreters of sacred lore decided that Enoch's reminiscences must have been some kind of "parable" or "vision"? But we're not living in the Dark Ages anymore. How many more arguments does it need to bring these backwoodsmen out of their woods? And bear in mind that everything that I, the diligent chronicler of today, am typing into my computer right now is nothing new; it's thousands of years old! Just forgotten, twisted, misinterpreted, and repressed. It's about time that the old texts were presented in a modern, comprehensible form to make it possible to plumb their meanings. May doubt shatter the old authorities, and reason triumph over faith.

From scientific circles we learn that research must first concentrate on the most easily reachable and plausible explanations before reaching for more exotic solutions. In that case, what is the closest, most sensible solution when looking at the Enoch texts? To be sure, it's not what we have gotten from previous exegesis. Those interpretations make no sense because they are based on God and his archangels and angels as some kind of executive body. Then this almighty creator of the universe is credited with deeds that would be absolutely beneath a true god. The simplest means of extracting the real sense of the text is to look at it from a contemporary standpoint. And that is indeed the intention of the "lord" who ordered the dictation of the books: "And he said unto me: 'Observe, Enoch, these heavenly tablets, read what is written thereon, and mark you well every single fact.' And I observed the heavenly tablets, and read everything which was written thereon and understood everything, and read the book...." (Chapter 81, 1 ff)[62]

Before his final journey into the heavens, this same Enoch, writer of the Lord's word, passed these books on to his son: "Preserve, my son Methuselah, the books thou hast received from thy father's hand, and deliver them to the generations of the world...."[63]

If it turns out that the Egyptians are indeed right, and Enoch is the same person as Saurid, the pyramid builder, then there could well be some pretty amazing surprises lying in wait for us within the Great Pyramid. After all, Al-Maqrizi stressed in the *Khitat* that texts were placed in the pyramids "to protect them and preserve them."[64] Science is based on the creation of knowledge. As far as the Great Pyramid of Giza is concerned, science has practiced exactly the opposite. The Egyptologists of the present day—at least the Arabs among them—should read the texts of their forefathers, too. One can read in the *Khitat* that Saurid (alias Enoch) had decorated the interior of the eastern pyramid (allegedly the Cheops Pyramid) with "the various canopies of the skies and the planets,"[65] in addition to "books about the stars. Also the fixed stars and that which betakes to happen from time to time...as well as the events of the past...."[66]

None of this is known to the Egyptologists. The Cheops Pyramid is totally anonymous—not one single glyph remains on its walls. But wait! In the Grand Gallery, the grandiose entrance hall to the "King's Chamber," there are large metal brackets that are mentioned nowhere in the scholarly literature. It could well be that these brackets were once holders for gold panels and that, in ancient times, the Grand Gallery was a fantastic stairway to the "King's Chamber," flanked left and right with the tidings from the past. Bands of grave robbers may well have taken these panels and melted them down. Yet there are other possibilities. As is now fairly widely known, within and beneath the so-called Cheops Pyramid lie various shafts and rooms.[67,68] But despite this, the holier-than-thou antiquities administration in Cairo wants none of this to be made public.

The Fallen Angels

The real drama in the Book of Enoch, however, takes place between the ship's captain—"the Most High" in the religious interpretation—and his crew—the "fallen angels." This group of beings does the one thing that angels never could:

> And it came to pass when the children of men had multiplied, that in those days were born unto them beautiful and comely daughters. But when the angels, the children of the heaven, saw them they lusted after them, and said to one another: "Come, let us choose us wives from among the children of men and beget us children." And Semjaza, who was their leader, said unto them: "I fear ye will not indeed agree to do this deed, and I alone shall have to pay the penalty

of a great sin." And they all answered him and said: "Let us all swear an oath, and all bind ourselves by mutual imprecations not to abandon this plan but to do this thing." Then they all swore together and bound themselves by mutual imprecations upon it. And they were in number two hundred, who descended in the days of Jared upon the summit of Mount Hermon.

(Chapter 6, 1–6)[69]

And you need some kind of major theological song and dance to explain that? The facts are presented plainly enough: a crew of two hundred "sons of heaven" land on Mont Hermon, find themselves surrounded by beautiful earthly maidens, and decide they want to do what comes naturally. But because this forbidden, they make a pact that they will all see it through and will not let anything keep them from their aims. Sex between people and extraterrestrials has been dealt with before in other articles.[70] And there is also, of course, the case of the angel named *Samael* who seduced the mother of man, Eve: "...and lo he looked not as the earthly, but rather as the heavenly."[71] Other crew members tucked into the delicious earthly maidens—and even lads—with gusto. To the horror of the Bible believers, it is even reported in the Book of Books:

"When men began to increase in number on the earth and daughters were born to them, the sons of God saw that the daughters of men were beautiful, and they married any of them they chose."[72]

You can read it for yourself in the first Book of Moses—Genesis, chapter 6, verses 1 and 2.

As long as theology has been around as a science, there has been a fierce debate about what the phrase "sons of God" actually means, and the resulting thousands of pages of commentaries on the subject are highly contradictory. One school of thought claims that it means "giants," whereas others are equally convinced that it means "God's children," "fallen angels," "apostate spirits." It's enough to make you scream! One simple Bible phrase turns faith on its head! But actually, anyone who has studied Hebrew and knows the characters of the alphabet and their meaning knows exactly what these syllables express: "Those who fell from the sky [were] manlike beings of great size."[73]

I can only manage a resigned smile for this academic feud. After all, however you interpret this biblical passage, something's going to come out wrong. If you take "sons of God" literally, then it means that God must have had children—and all that in the age of Adam! And *they* had sex with the daughters of men. It's unthinkable! If the phrase means "fallen angels," there must have been some kind of conflict in Heaven. What? In God's heavenly presence? But there must have been some kind of a blowup, or there wouldn't be any "fallen angels." There's only one really sensible way of understanding what was meant: extraterrestrials. Basta! And it becomes even clearer when Enoch lists the names of the ringleaders: "And these are the names of their leaders: Semjaza, their leader, Araklba, Rameel, Kokablel, Tamlel, Ramlel, Danel, Ezeqeel, Baraqijal, Asael, Armaros, Batarel, Ananel, Zaqiel, Samsapeel, Satarel, Turel, Jomjael, Sariel." (Chapter 6, verses 7 and 8. Note: The names in this list vary according to which version of the text you read.)[74]

And this group of beings doesn't sit around when they get here. Enoch describes their deeds:

> And Asael taught men to make swords, and knives, and shields, and breastplates, and made known to them the metals of the earth and the art of working them, and bracelets, and ornaments, and the use of antimony, and the beautifying of the eyelids, and all kinds of costly stones, and all coloring tinctures...Semjaza taught enchantments, and root cuttings...Baraqijal taught astrology, Kokabel the constellations, Ezeqeel the knowledge of the clouds, Araqiel the signs of the earth, Shamsiel the signs of the sun, and Sariel the course of the moon...."
> (Chapter 8)[75]

The list of names is not complete: there were 200 "fallen angels" in all who descended onto Mount Hermon all those thousands of years ago. So what about all the others? Enoch does provide us with another list; after all, he could write and he understood their language. The strangers themselves had taught him. So Enoch took on the role of interpreter between the ETs and his own folk.

> And these are their names:
>
> The first of them is Semjaza,
>
> the second Artaqifa,
>
> and the third Armen,
>
> the fourth Kokabel,
>
> the fifth Turael,
>
> the sixth Rumjal,
>
> the seventh Danjal,
>
> the eighth Neqael,
>
> the ninth Baraqijal,
>
> the tenth Azazel,
>
> the eleventh Armaros,
>
> the twelfth Batarjal,
>
> the thirteenth Busasejal,
>
> the fourteenth Hananel,
>
> the fifteenth Turel,
>
> and the sixteenth Simapesiel,
>
> the seventeenth Jetrel,
>
> the eighteenth Tumael,
>
> the nineteenth Turel,
>
> the twentieth Rumael,
>
> the twenty-first Azazael.[76]

And these are the names of their chief ones over hundreds, fifties, and tens:

> The name of the first Jeqon: who was the one who led astray [all] the sons of God, and brought them down to the earth, and led them astray through the daughters of men. And the second was named Asbeel: he imparted to the holy sons of God evil counsel, and led them astray so that they defiled their bodies with the daughters of men. And the third was named Gadreel: he it is who showed the children of men all the blows of death, and he led astray Eve, and showed the weapons of death to the sons of men: the shield and the coat of mail, and the sword for battle, and all the weapons of death to the children of men. And from his hand they have proceeded against those who dwell on the earth from that day and for evermore. And the fourth was named Penemue: he taught the children of men the bitter and the sweet, and he taught them all the secrets of their wisdom. *And he also instructed mankind in writing with ink and paper....*[author's italics]
> (Chapter 69, 2 ff)[77]

This passage says it all—we can all read it. But the problem with our society is that most people are too lazy to think; it's too much for them; they are so exhausted that they need people to think for them so that they can work their way up in life.

Up to No Good

Enoch's list not only gives us the names of those renegade angels who "descended to Mount Hermon"—this sounds to me *very much* like a mutinous crew—it also provides us with several of the professions of these "watchers of heaven," as they are called in one passage. Jeqon is revealed to be some kind of ringleader who convinces his colleagues to have sex with the fair earthly maidens. Asbeel helps him. Gadreel and, in the earlier list, Asael seemed to be warlike metallurgists who first show man how to smelt metal and then how to manufacture breastplates, shields, and battle swords—

which begs the question, of course: where were the enemies that needed fighting with these weapons? Penemue, the teacher of the crew, taught not only writing with pen and ink, he also instructed mankind on the finesses of nutrition. Baraqijal turned out to be an astronomer; Kokabal was an astrologer—a science that means little to us these days; Ezeqeel was a meteorologist ("the knowledge of the clouds"); Araqiel was a geologist; and so on. From my contemporary viewpoint, it seems like a part of the crew rebelled against the "Most High," the "Great Glory" (the starship commander), and they knew full well that there was no going back. So they did their best to survive on Earth and teach the Stone Age Earthlings how to make weapons and other useful objects that they hadn't known previously. This scenario is not mine: it's exactly how Enoch describes it.

After the 200 "watchers of heaven" came down and satisfied their sexual lusts on Earth, they suddenly started getting nervous that the captain would blow his top. So they sent Enoch up to the mother ship, hoping that, as an Earthling, he could put in a good word or two for them:

> [They] lifted me upward, and bore me into heaven. And I went in till I drew nigh to a wall built of crystals and surrounded by tongues of fire: and it began to scare me. And I went into the tongues of fire and approached a large house which was built of crystals. The walls of the house were like a tiled floor made of crystals, and its foundation was also of crystal. Its ceiling was like the path of the stars and the lightnings, and between them were fiery cherubim, and their heaven was as water. A flaming fire surrounded the walls, and its portals blazed with fire.... There was a second house, greater than the former, and all its doors stood open before me, and it was built of flames of fire. And in every respect it so excelled in splendor and magnificence and extent that I cannot describe to you its splendor and its extent. And its floor was of fire, and above it were lightnings and the path of the stars, and its ceiling also was blazing fire. And I looked and saw therein a lofty throne: its appearance was as crystal, and the wheels thereof as the shining sun.... And the Great Glory sat thereon, and His raiment shone more brightly than the sun and was whiter than any snow. (Chapter 14, 9-21)[78]

An Arbitrary Chronology

Critics may well point out here that I haven't actually quoted these passages from the Book of Enoch in the "right" order and am thus deliberately distorting the chronology of events. Well, I beg your pardon! The ordering of the chapters by the experts of previous ages was random in itself. No one was in a position to say with any great certainty in what order the various parchments and scrolls were meant to be read. They set to their task with great enthusiasm, trying to make order out of chaos based on their idea of what the text was trying to say. As translator Dr. Emil Kautzsch noted in 1900, the text is "not from a single source."[79] And because not one single expert from more than a century ago was capable of really identifying what it was really about, Dr. Kautzsch also asked himself: "What have these broadly spun theories [from Enoch] about the sun, moon, stars, winds and similar subjects got to do with the messianic judgment?"[80] Every Enoch translator, without exception, has had to deal with exactly the same dilemma. The order of the texts has never been fully understood. On the one hand, this is because new extracts were always being added that upset the chronology and, on the other, because words and expressions could be interpreted in wildly differing ways. Only the Slavonic Book of Enoch exists in three different variants: the long, medium, and short recensions. In the longer edit, experts have no difficulty in identifying the different handwriting styles of five different scribes using Middle-Bulgarian orthography. One South Russian handwriting style can even be pinpointed to the city of its origin: "written in the city of Poltava in the imperial church of the resurrection of our Lord God and Savior Jesus Christ...in the monastery of the Ascension of our Lord."[81] Alongside this, there are Serbian and Russian Enoch texts, one consisting of 189 folios and the other of 362. Like the so-called urtexts of the gospels of the New Testament, these versions of Enoch have been edited from time to time. The abbots and monks believed that these books referred to the messiah, redemptions, the final judgment, and the second coming of the Messiah, not to mention the divine judgment of the apocalypse (as mentioned in the "Revelations" of the New Testament). Logically, passages from the original text that made no sense were adapted to fit the thinking of the day. What chaos! In this way, parts of the "longer version" translated by Dr. Nathanael Bonwetsch turned out differently to the Greek or Slavonic variants. For instance, in this description of the descent of the "watchers of heaven" [82]: "...they went down on to earth from the Lord's throne, to the place Ermon, and broke through their vows on the shoulder of the hill Ermon and saw the daughters of men how good they are, and took to themselves wives, and befouled the earth with their deeds...." (Chapter XVII)[83]

The logic of the respectable analysts of the last 200 years simply doesn't add up. Their ideas, which still guide thinking even today, were wrong from the very beginning. Any other possible interpretations were suffocated at the start by a tightly tied religious corset that gave them no room to breathe. Lines were drawn that were not to be crossed. And, as far as our contemporary interpretation is concerned, perhaps we are being a bit unfair to our forebears, who could hardly have been expected to know of interstellar travel. This contemporary viewpoint changes the entire meaning of Enoch—and not just Enoch! The consequences could be highly disquieting, for the very existence of extraterrestrials generally, let alone thousands of years ago, forces us to draw conclusions that blow our current view of things to pieces. And I'm not saying this from arrogance or even as a joke. There's simply no way around it: we have to re-interpret the texts that we have received from our ancestors from a modern viewpoint. There are too many of them to ignore. They are scattered everywhere around the world, and more will come from the ruins and the temples (you, my dear reader, will find out more in the next chapter), such as the Voynich manuscript. We are marching in a straight line directly into the age of wonders and awakening. Human history is not over yet—not by a long way.

A Voyage Into the Heavens

Enoch experiences, as do Abraham, Ezekiel, Arjuna, and Enkidu in other histories, a journey into space—a journey that he is simply not equipped to comprehend. And his astonishment does not abate. He knows nothing of the materials used to construct the spaceship. So for him, the heat-resistant tiles of the hull are bright crystals, and the reinforced glass and holographic displays are a "ceiling like the path of the stars."[84] Awestruck and afraid, he is led to see the captain: "the Great Glory sat [on his throne], and His raiment shone more brightly than the sun and was whiter than any snow."[85] And what does this glorious deity do? He greets Enoch and makes it clear that the "fallen angels"—the mutineers—can expect nothing more from him:

> Fear not, Enoch, thou righteous man and scribe of righteousness. Approach hither and hear my voice. And go, say to the watchers of heaven, who have sent thee to intercede for them: "You should intercede" for men, and not men for you: Wherefore have ye left the high, holy, and eternal heaven, and lain with women, and defiled yourselves with the daughters of men and taken to yourselves wives, and done like the children of earth...?
> (Chapter 15, 1–4)[86]

The "Great Glory" also knows how he is going to deal with his mutinous crew and their offspring: a terrible flood over all the Earth. "Yea, there shall come a great destruction over the whole earth, and there shall be a deluge...and there shall be a great punishment on the earth, and the earth shall be cleansed from all impurity." (Chapter 106, 13 ff)[87] In the longer recension, this passage goes into more detail: "And for that reason, I shall bring down a flood on the Earth, and the Earth itself will be destroyed and sink into mud."[88]

Having said that, the "Great Glory" takes steps to ensure that a select few survive, so that, over the course of the millennia, the human population will be in a position to recover—until his return. In the long recension of the Slavonic Book of Enoch, the "Great Glory" speaks of a "second coming." Interestingly, the survivors of the flood carry a changed genetic structure.

This can clearly be deduced from the ancient writings, and I've written about it extensively in my other books.[89,90] (And the clever geneticists will be able to see for themselves!)

Is it even permissible to deduce a single Enoch from this confusion of Enoch texts, and then on top of that to—arbitrarily?—filter out those passages that fit in with a modern interpretation? Just to remind you: Enoch himself stresses his authorship many times as Methuselah's father. Then knowledge is dictated to him that simply cannot be ascribed to any antediluvian society:

"And I saw other lightnings and the stars of heaven.... And I saw *how they are weighed in a righteous balance, according to their proportions of light, the width of their spaces and the day of their appearing.*" [author's italics] (Chapter 43, 1–2) [91]

How do today's astronomers classify the stars? They also have a classification system that is based on magnitude ("weighed in a righteous balance"), brightness ("according to their proportions of light"), relative position ("the width of their spaces"), as well as the date of their discovery ("the day of their appearing"). The antediluvian Enoch must have received such sound information from his source that was way ahead of his times. These strange instructors—in the Book of Enoch they are named as *Uriel* and *Pravuil*—dictate and demonstrate astronomical and meteorological knowledge of great sophistication to the dumbstruck Enoch. To us it might seem like pretty everyday stuff, but not to someone in Enoch's time:

> And there mine eyes saw the secrets of the lightning and of the thunder, and the secrets of the winds, how they are divided to blow over the earth, and the secrets of the clouds and dew.... And I saw the chambers of the sun and moon, whence they proceed and whither they come again, and their glorious return, and how one is superior to the other, and their stately orbit, and how they do not leave their orbit, and they add nothing to their orbit and they take nothing from it.... And after that I saw the hidden and the visible path of the moon, and how she accomplishes the course of her path in that place by day and by night.... (Chapter 41, 3 ff) And after that all the secrets of

the lights and lightnings were shown to me, and they lighten for blessing and for satisfying the Earth.... (Chapter 59, 3) For the thunder has places of rest assigned to it while it is waiting for its peal; and the thunder and lightning are inseparable, and although not one and undivided, they both go together through the spirit and separate not. For when the lightning lightens, the thunder utters its voice...." (Chapter 61, 14–15)[92]

Enoch learns things that we didn't learn until thousands of years later through arduous research. He writes of the "hidden path of the moon" and laws regarding thunder and lightning which are truly hard to credit to a stone-age society. The angel Uriel teaches him about a "treasury of lights and thunder" (Chapter 17, 3)[93], which is pretty hard for Enoch to grasp. After all, the mere concept of a "treasury of thunder" is not something that just comes to you while riding on the back of a camel. In an orbiting space station, on the other hand, astronauts view the "treasury of thunder" on a daily basis. It is the gigantic reservoir of electrical charge that builds up in the variously charged levels of cloud and comes down from the storm to the Earth like "columns of heavenly fire" (Enoch again).

Intergalactic Astronomy Lessons

Enoch's instruction includes the sun, the moon, the leap years, and the paths of the stars in relation to the Earth's rotation. Wow! Seeing as books about Enoch cannot generally be found in most bookstores and the Internet has little more than superficial commentaries that don't add anything to our understanding, I can offer little more than a few quotes from Charles's more-than-100-year-old translation:

> The book of the courses of the luminaries of the heaven, the relations of each, according to their classes, their dominion and their seasons, according to their names and places of origin, and according to their months, which Uriel, the holy angel, who was with me, who is their guide, showed me.... And first there goes forth the great luminary,

named the Sun, and his circumference is like the circumference of the heaven, and he is quite filled with illuminating and heating fire...and the sun goes down from the heaven and returns through the north in order to reach the east.... When the sun rises in the heaven, he comes forth through that fourth portal thirty, mornings in succession, and sets accurately in the fourth portal in the west of the heaven. And during this period the day becomes daily longer and the night nightly shorter....
(Chapter 72, 1 ff)[94]

And it goes on in the same vein: the sun travels through these imaginary "portals," and the days get longer and the nights get shorter until "[o]n that day the day is equalized with the night, and the night amounts to nine parts and the day to nine parts." (Chapter 72, 20-21)[95]

Anyone can see that the sun rises in the east and sets in the west. But these sunrises and sunsets don't always take place at exactly the same locations. The point at which the sun rises and sets shifts every day within a set of fixed boundaries, which are dependent on the point of observation. On the first days of spring (March 21st) and fall (September 23rd) the sun rises exactly in the east and sets exactly in the west. On every other day the sunrise and sunset are a little offset from these points. These are Enoch's "portals," in which the sun travels. Until the displacement is again canceled out, as Enoch confirms: "And the sun has therewith traversed the divisions of his orbit and turns again on those divisions of his orbit." (Chapter 72, 27)[96]

I believe in evolution—with certain reservations—and swallowed my Enoch with the appropriate amount of healthy skepticism. It is simply impossible that modern knowledge crops up in ancient books and our "super-clever" philologists, theologians, and exegetes make "visions" or "Enoch's magic garden" out of it. Sometimes I feel like I'm in some kind of weird ballet. Nymphs are dancing all around me on tiptoe, accompanied by effeminate men in flowing robes, and they are all weaving a picture of a fantastic world that doesn't even exist. Do *none* of these people have any imagination? Or are they just incapable of throwing off the ballast of the previous generations?

I tend to describe myself as a imaginative realist, but I don't let my imagination run away with me. The boundaries between today's realists—the scientists—and my way of looking at things are not fixed. It's just that the scientist turns away as soon as reality takes on a fantastic form. For us today, Enoch's reality is still pretty fantastic—as it was indeed for Enoch himself. I remember a scientist once saying to me after a talk show about aliens that we had both participated in: "These aren't the sort of things that we should be worrying about! We should be looking at our own current problems!" He didn't want to believe that the past had a strong influence on our present. If ETs really did visit our planet millennia ago and passed on their knowledge to someone like Enoch, that's got plenty to do with right now. Just think, my dear reader, about the impact on religion, the philosophical consequences, the possibilities for space flight technology that can cross light years, or think about the ancient promise of a second coming that crops up in practically every religion to this present day. Obviously, there are two types of hypotheses: the embarrassing ones and the rest. Enoch's instructors—call them "angels" if you like, although it doesn't really fit the picture—knew perfectly well *why* they were teaching their pupil:

> The smaller luminary, which is named the Moon...her rising and setting change every month: and her days are like the days of the sun, and when her light is uniform [i.e. full] it amounts to the seventh part of the light of the sun. And thus she rises. And her first phase in the east comes forth on the thirtieth morning: and on that day she becomes visible, and constitutes for you the first phase of the moon.... And the one half of her goes forth by a seventh part, and her whole circumference is empty, without light, with the exception of one-seventh part of it, and the fourteenth part of her light.... And all these Uriel, the holy angel who is the leader of them all, showed to me, and their positions, and I wrote down their positions as he showed them to me.... In single seventh parts she accomplishes all her light in the east, and in single seventh parts accomplishes all her darkness in the west....
> (Chapters 73-74)[97]

In the modern publication *Handbook of Space,* you can read exactly the same thing:

> The point at which the moon crosses the plane of the ecliptic from south to north is called the rising node, the other is called the falling node.... The most striking thing about the moon's appearance is its phases. As the moon itself has no source of luminescence, but rather simply reflects the light of the sun, the phases of the moon are dependent on the relative positions of these two heavenly bodies....[98]

This just paraphrases the information that we hear from Enoch, only he speaks of "portals" in which the sun and the moon move. He also describes the phases of the moon, and he knows that the Earth's satellite receives its light from the sun. Statements such as these presuppose two things: that the observer realizes not only that the Earth is a sphere, but also that it follows an elliptic path around the sun. Somehow that doesn't fit in with my preconceptions of the state of scientific thinking in the third century B.C., the period in which the Book of Enoch was supposedly written. Johannes Keppler, Galileo Galilei, and Sir Isaac Newton all came onto the scene a lot later. In Chapters 74 and 75, Enoch provides a description of the leap days:

> And if five years are added together the sun has a surplus of thirty days, and all the days which accrue to it for one of those five years, when they are full, amount to 364 days.... And the leaders...have also to do with the four intercalary days, being inseparable from their office, according to the reckoning of the year, and these render service on the four days which are not reckoned in the reckoning of the year.... For the signs and the times and the years and the days the angel Uriel showed to me.... And I saw chariots in the heaven, running in the world, above those portals *in which revolve the stars that never set.* And one is larger than all the rest, and it is that that makes its course through the entire world. [author's italics][99]

Echoes From India

When I read that Enoch has seen "chariots in the heaven, running in the world, above those portals in which revolve the stars that never set," then my thoughts are drawn to ancient India. Take a look at this:

> Indra's car, endued with great effulgence and driven by Matali, came dividing the clouds and illuminating the firmament, filling the entire sky with its roar. It was a heavenly creation, blinding to behold. Arjuna—blazing like the Sun—himself ascended the celestial car.... As he approached that realm invisible to the mortals of the Earth, he beheld thousands of cars of extraordinary beauty. And in that region there was no sun or moon or fire to give light.... And those brilliant regions that are seen from the Earth in the form of stars, like lamps, are great heavenly bodies....[100]

It simply does not make sense to analyze Enoch's tales in isolation, or to view them solely in terms of their relation to other semi-religious, wishy-washy texts belonging to the Judaeo-Christian faith, and just sweep the rest under the carpet! But there's light at the end of the tunnel—even if it's light coming from thousands of years in the past. The state of our knowledge today is not the peak of wisdom, and mankind is not the pinnacle of evolution. Our stubborn belief in the findings of scientists is only justifiable in areas where science is an exact art. All deductions based on collected wisdom, however, must be treated with caution and questioned as soon as new information comes to light. The information provided by these ancient texts is neither reverie nor wishful thinking; it is there, and it will confound and astonish our Internet-surfing society into more chaos than even the invention of the radio.

Even today, we live in a kind of puzzling dream world: the TV screen is like a magic mirror that brings us pictures of military maneuvers in Iraq, political events from Peru, or expeditions to the South Pole—all delivered to our living rooms at the touch of a button. We experience the assassination of a U.S. president and then, just a short time later, we see the same man—risen from the dead it seems—talking and smiling at us from the flickering screen. We watch science programs showing discoveries made under the microscope, and we never know what is truth and what is simply propaganda. We gape at rocket launches and stare in wonder at the International Space Station that's buzzing by somewhere over our heads, shining like a weak star. When the planet Earth finally shakes off its infestation of human beings, heaven alone knows how our successors on this world will describe the past. Just imagine, dear reader, that some catastrophe were to hit the Earth—it doesn't matter what. But somewhere, on the peak of some isolated Swiss Alp, a ragged few have somehow survived. You can rest assured that they would do everything they could to ensure that the species survived and start producing children as soon as possible. And one proud father, sitting with his son on his knee, would look up as an excessively large, mutated mountain eagle soared by their cabin:

"Look, son," the father would say, pointing. "When I was younger there were metal birds hundreds of times larger than that eagle. And people could sit in the belly of the bird and look out of windows onto the Earth below. These mighty birds flew faster than an arrow over the great water to a place where houses were built so high they reached up into the clouds...."

The father grows old and dies, and the son himself becomes a father. Now, the young father retells the story for his young son:

"Just imagine, my son. Your grandfather told me that there were once giant birds in which people could sit and look down at the Earth beneath them. These birds flew faster than any arrow and could even cross the mighty water to a place where the houses grew up into the clouds...."

Already by the second generation, the story is unfeasible. So just try and imagine what happens when, many generations later, theologians try and analyze these scenes from their religio-psychological standpoint. Holy Enoch help us!

Today, you can find many texts from long-forgotten epochs, even if they've been rewritten many times and adapted to meet the understanding of the age. Some of these texts have been intentionally transformed into ciphers, such as the Jewish Cabbala, so that only a selected circle of the initiated can understand the encrypted contents. Other, like the Popol Vuh or the Mayan inscriptions—there are three versions!—only remain in small excerpts, and even then probably poorly translated at that. And then there are those, such as the Voynich manuscript, that defy any attempt at all to reveal their contents. It's hardly worth mentioning all of the hundreds of thousands of writings that have fallen victim to fire or intentional destruction over the centuries. But the Bible, the Apocrypha, and good old Enoch's book all really do exist, even if they are no longer quite in their original forms. What do we make of them, we oh-so-clever modern men and women? We transform an intentional genetic mutation, in other words a change in our genetic code, into a "miracle of birth." You can find in chapters 106 and 107 of the Book of Enoch, or in the Lamech Scroll, one of the famed "Dead Sea Scrolls."[101] And what do we clowns make of it? The original motif for the "immaculate conception"! The highly precise descriptions by the prophet Ezekiel in the Bible are transformed into "visions, dreams, inspirations" and other such humbug, although he is clearly talking about a shuttle craft. And we tinker around with the Book of Enoch, making it into some kind of incredible "magic garden." Mad!

A Legacy for Future Generations

The story of the seventh antediluvian king, "who ascended into heaven" as the scrolls say, has been falsified, adapted, expanded, changed, rewritten, and religiously interpreted, but the content is nevertheless still recognizable. And because this "seventh" appears both in the Jewish Torah and the

Old Testament under the name Enoch, this mixed bag of tales is collected together under the heading "the Books of Enoch." Even though the writer may well have been named something else entirely, I'm left with little option than to call him Enoch myself. This fellow was taught many branches of science by an alien race, and, to make things move along quicker, he learned to write using "a reed of quick-writing." After his heavenly crash course he was returned to his people with an urgent task: to teach them and to pass on his books so that they would survive the ages:

> And two thousand men came together and came to the place Achuzan where Enoch was with his sons. And the elders of the people, the whole assembly, came and bowed down and began to kiss Enoch and said to him: ...the Lord chose thee rather than all men on earth and designated thee writer of all his creation.
> (Chapter XLIV, 4–5, longer recension)[102]

Where is this place "Achuzan" where Enoch gathers his people? The astronomical information he provides give us a good basis for working it out. Before Enoch returns to "heaven"—or, in the modern version, to the mother ship to take the grand tour of space—he expends a great deal of effort in telling his folk all that has happened to him and to preserve his books for future generations:

> Enoch was born on the sixth day of the month Tsivan, and lived three hundred and sixty-five years. He was taken up to heaven on the first day of the month Tsivan and remained in heaven sixty days. He wrote all these signs of all creation, which the Lord created, and wrote three hundred and sixty-six books, and handed them over to his sons and remained on earth thirty days, and was again taken up to heaven on the sixth day of the month Tsivan, on the very day and hour when he was born.... Methuselah and his brethren, all the sons of Enoch, made haste, and erected an altar at the place called Achuzan, whence and where Enoch had been taken up to heaven."
> (Chapter LXVIII, longer recension)[103]

And if there remain any doubts as to whether it really was the seventh antediluvian patriarch Enoch and whether it was really books that were being talked about:

> "...Mark well the words of your father, which are all come to you from the Lord's lips. Take these books of your father's handwriting and read them....
> (Chapter XLVII, longer recension)[104]

> "Enoch indeed wrote this complete doctrine of wisdom...."
> (Chapter 92, 1)[105]

> "Another book which Enoch wrote for his son Methuselah and for those who will come after him...."
> (Chapter 108, 1)[106]

> "And after that Enoch both gave and began to recount from the books."
> (Chapter 93, 1)[107]

> "And now, my son Methuselah, call to me all thy brothers And gather together to me all the sons of thy mother...."
> (Chapter 91, 1)[108]

> "And now, my son, I have shown thee everything, and the law of all the stars of the heaven is completed."
> (Chapter 79, 1)[109]

> "And Methuselah made haste, and summoned his brethren, Regim, Riman, Uchan, Chermion, Gaidad, and all the elders of the people before the face of his father Enoch...."
> (Chapter LVII, 2)[110]

And we mustn't leave out his task for the future, because that includes us, too:

> "And now, my son Methuselah.... I have revealed to thee everything, and given thee books concerning all these: so preserve, my son Methuselah, *the books from thy father's hand, and see that thou deliver them to the generations of the world....*"
> [author's italics] (Chapter 82)[111]

Where are these books? The bundles of old parchments that make up the so-called Books of Enoch are certainly not what is meant. Sometime and somewhere these missing texts are going to turn up. This is what the "Great Glory" prophesies—and he ought to know:

> Behold from their seed shall arise another generation, much later, but of them many will be very insatiate. He who raises that generation, shall reveal to them the books of thy handwriting, of thy fathers, to them to whom he must point out the guardianship of the world, to the faithful men and workers of my pleasure, who do not acknowledge my name in vain. And they shall tell another generation, *and those others having read shall be glorified thereafter, more than those before.* [author's italics] (Chapter XXXV)[112]

Fantastic, these pearls of wisdom from days of yore! The diagnosis is a fitting one. Texts, which are simply too complex for the people in Enoch's times, will turn up thousands of years later, and those who read them will be "glorified thereafter, more than those before." Someone like me, who tends to look a little further back into the mists of time, might be of help in speeding along this time of awakening. A big change is coming, and politicians, self-important scientists, and unctuously blathering religious leaders may want to, but will never be able to, stop it. There is no vaccination against thinking. Ideas know no boundaries and no censorship. And what's more, ideas have a dangerous tendency to spread like wildfire.

The Miracle of Misinformation

The marvel of television is one means that is being used to try and turn society into a uniform mush. The manipulation and thought control inexorably continues. Mankind is being rinsed out into a group of dull moralists who convince themselves that they are "good people." Their view of the world is fabricated by the mass media, and the bosses and chief editors of the electronic media are just the henchmen for unnecessary "councils," "advisory boards" of political commissions, and "contingents," who don't miss a single chance to get involved in things—regardless of whether or not they have a clue what they're talking about. TV programs with opinions that contradict any religion—regardless of which one—are not permitted. That's what we've come to!

Our unscientific nature, our faith in some rubbish or other, dominates our lives. The massive flood of information out there has just made us sluggish. We'd rather vegetate in front of the TV than read a book with an attentive and critical eye, rather laze on the beach in Hurghada than take a closer look at the Great Pyramid. Today's young people mess around with their computers; their monitors spew out data that interests no one and is therefore immediately consigned to the trashcan of forgetfulness. What does it help us in this electronic age to have thousands of times the amount of information available if nothing ever gets done with it? Yes, we surf through it, but we never really dive in. The Internet manipulates *us,* because we believe that we can call up just about anything we want and that makes us well-informed. IT = Information Trickery. The Net only spits out what somebody somewhere else has typed in. So you'll find it hard, dear reader, to find either apocryphal texts, or *Manetho's* list of Egyptian kings, not to mention the complete translation of *Mahabharata* by Chandra Roy from 1888. Much of what we "know" about the Net is an illusion. We are fumbling around in the dark when we go looking for ancient texts that are never likely to end up online. Giga: garbage in, garbage out. So there will never be any cross-indexing. The omniscient Internet is one-sided and basically already a manipulation of those who believe that they can rely on it, entered for the like-minded among the like-minded.

Today's "mouse potatoes" behave like all people who think along the same lines, from the very moment they sit down at the keyboard. Just like semiconscious patients all twitching in time with each other. It doesn't even shock me anymore, because I know how the system works. There are no cross-linkages outside of the Net; they're simply unknown. Thus a kind of psychosis of faith has arisen—you could almost describe it as a culture of hangers-on—which has become routine in our allegedly so-well-informed society. Connecting the past with the future is unthinkable for single-track minds. But the two are nevertheless utterly intertwined, and anyone who hasn't figured that out yet had better learn quickly, because the future is about to be overrun by the past. How are we going to behave when Enoch's alien friends actually return? And *that* they are going to return is as sure as night follows day. For those who are interested I recommend my book *Der Götter-Schock* (*The God Shock*). Are we going to suffer a god shock? The fact that our thinking is manipulated from the moment of our births is illustrated nicely (or nastily, if you prefer) in the following example that has stuck in my mind since hearing a lecture by Professor Karl Steinbuch some 40 years ago: In one country children are brought up to be churchgoers; in another to be Muslims. And neither society considers that simply switching the babies can make an otherwise Christian child a Muslim, or vice versa. This simple insight demonstrates the fundamental nature of any indoctrination.

After Enoch learned the language of the extraterrestrials, having been taught by "angels," and wrote everything down on parchment with his "a reed of quick-writing," and then spent 30 days relating the whole episode to his sons and eldest, his new, "heavenly" friends come and fetch him for the *grand tour.* The people don't understand what is going on:

> When Enoch had talked to the people, the Lord sent out darkness on to the earth, and there was darkness, and it covered those men standing with Enoch, and they took Enoch up on to the highest heaven.... And the people who saw but understood not how Enoch bad been taken, glorified God, and all went to their homes.
> (Chapter LXVII, longer recension)[113]

Enoch Takes His Leave

The Ancient Legends of the Jews tell a somewhat longer version of Enoch's disappearance. The "angels," they claim, had promised Enoch to take him with them, but the departure had not been finally decided: "A call came to me that I would depart to heaven, yet I knew not on which day I would go from you."[114] So Enoch and his people sit around, and he imparts to them all he has learned from the angels *Uriel* and *Pravuil.* In particular, he stresses to them that his books must not be kept secret, but must be retained for the future generations (something I approve of!). After a few days of teaching, it starts getting exciting:

> And it occurred at the same time as the people and Enoch sat and Enoch spoke to them. The people lifted up their eyes and saw the figure of a steed descend from heaven, and the steed rode down on a storm to Earth. And the people told Enoch what they saw: "This steed has come down for me. The time has come and the day that I must go from among you and never see you again." Then the steed was there and all saw it clearly.[115]

Apparently Enoch had been forewarned by the ETs Uriel and Pravuil that the takeoff would be dangerous for any bystanders, so he advised his followers to withdraw. He warned the curious onlookers many times not to follow him "so that you do not die."[116] Some of them understood, but the most obstinate spectators were desperate to witness Enoch's "rapture" first-hand. It gets dramatic: "They spoke, we will follow you to the place from whence you depart; only death can stand between us. And because they were stubborn he spoke no more with them and they followed him and did not turn back. And so it happened: Enoch ascended in weather into the stormy heaven on fiery steeds in a fiery chariot."[117]

Enoch's trip into the clouds ends fatally for his companions. On the following day, a search party goes out to find those who had accompanied the master:

And they sought at that place where Enoch had ascended to heaven and when they came to the site they found the ground blanketed in snow and great stones were as snow stones. They spoke to one another and said: Let us shovel away this snow to see if those who followed Enoch lie under it. And they shoveled away the snow and found those who had accompanied Enoch lying dead. They also sought Enoch, but they found him not, for he had ascended into heaven. This happened in one hundred thirteenth year of the life of Lamech, the son of Methuselah, as Enoch ascended into heaven."[118]

This dramatic finale must have left even the exegetes somewhat perplexed, as they have always interpreted Enoch's "ascension" as simply his acceptance into the bosom of God. Just imagine the dear, kindly God looks on indifferently as hundreds of innocent onlookers are burnt to a crisp while their teacher travels up to heaven? They listened to their wise Enoch, they honored him, they had attached themselves to him, and, finally, they fatally followed him to his launch site. What had these people really done wrong? Enoch departs "in weather" and "on fiery steeds in fiery chariots," but back on the ground all are burned alive—man and mouse—and even the stones are scorched white and are covered in a fine white powder that resembles snow. These days, we know that certain rocks (for instance, limestone) turn white when exposed to extreme heat and that sand—depending on the temperature—will fuse into glassy crystals that look like white salt. And our dear, loving God did that? And the theologians describe it all as Enochian "visions"? Didn't God have the power to fetch his pupil in a less-destructive manner? Why the agonizing and dramatic immolation of so many people, who simply wanted to accompany their beloved master Enoch?

Time for a New Take

Theology, philology, philosophy—these are, after all, humanities, and yet it is precisely these groups who accuse me and a few of my like-minded contemporaries of "warping" the texts to fit our theories. What kind of intellectual leaps do you need to make something divine out of the "Most High" and the "Great Glory" in the Books of Enoch? Admittedly, I have a certain amount of understanding for some of these old-school interpretations: after all, our honorable forefathers couldn't have been expected to have understood anything about interstellar travel and consequently comprehended, interpreted, and conserved the texts within their own theological frame of reference. But conservation is the same as preservation—and even the best preservatives can't keep the food fresh forever.

The Enoch texts and many other ancient documents are crying out for a more contemporary interpretation. But, in our society, they immediately cry out in shock and horror: "impossible," "flight of fancy," or even "sacrilege"! When will knowledge win through and people realize that the wheel of understanding is not turned by the accountants—even if they're academics—but by those who do not want to shut out understanding? As early as 1946, the UNO declared that the freedom of information was a fundamental human right. And all so-called "free" states have laws such as the "Freedom of Information Act," as it is called in the United States of America. The freedom to exchange information is one of the most valuable rights that we possess. Everyone should be free to say, write, and even print their opinions, it stands to reason. Doesn't it?

Even in the democratic world, we have already regressed to the stage where books are banned by law. A single person or a religious group—or even worse, a political ideology—feels hurt and is puffed up with indignation and, before you know it, the book is on the banned list (sometimes before it's even been published!), as if the affected parties were not capable of suing for libel, and the genuine or alleged cases of slander couldn't be put together properly. In some of the most extreme cases, this is at the cost of the author who trumpeted these "libels" into the world. These days, we've reached a point where certain things can no longer be said in public. They are impeded by political correctness or sanctimonious legislation that screams out for—can you believe it?—eavesdropping and spying to find out who said what. The judicially led manipulation, the Orwellian state, is being brought about a piece at a time by political clowns who take themselves unutterably seriously. And the poor judges, who have to push through this nonsense, convince themselves that their judgments contribute to the peace of mind of society and that is a higher aim than any constitution. As a member of the international PEN Club, which is committed to the freedom of speech and the written word, I am embarrassed to my ears about these unholy laws that restrict our freedom and that even now exist in my home country of Switzerland. It's amazing how far these political fools have come.

In a theocracy, there is no freedom of information. Those who forbid the spoken and written word always have reason to fear it. Its own indoctrination stinks to high heaven! Society is "adapted"—the next phase is like this: by the left, quick march!

I made the assertion that texts from extraterrestrials exist on the Earth and referred to the following examples:

The god Theuth gave the pharaoh writings in Naucratis.

The so-called Book of Adam preserved in a sapphire.

Oannes (in Babylon) gave the people a book.

The divine being *Yma* from the holy book of the Parsees, the *Avesta,* presented writings. The same being was known to the Phoenicians as *Taut.*

The Chinese emperor receives texts from a monster called *Meng-ho,* a beast with "the body of a horse and the head of a dragon."

The divine master *Padmasambhava* in Tibet brings indecipherable writings down to Earth that are being preserved to this very day for the time when "they can be understood."

Diodorus of Sicily claims that a god taught man how to read and write.

Enoch: "Observe, Enoch, these heavenly tablets, read what is written thereon...." Enoch is taught by angels and is given a "reed of quick-writing." He passes on his books to his son Methuselah.

My list isn't complete—thousands of authors from antiquity and scriptures from various religions have claimed the same thing. So, what do we do with it? Just fairy stories, nonsense, rubbish, visions, imaginings, wishful thinking, raptures, *magic gardens?* Or are we the problem? Is it our way of looking at things? Is it that we just can't believe what is staring us in the face? Our thinking is led by scholarly thinking from the moment we start in school. *Evolution* is the magic word. And the fact that evolution exists has been proven and is indisputable. With reservations. Not everything runs according to the happy evolution principle. There have been targeted genetic mutations throughout man's history. That can at least be proven by ancient writings, and those who don't believe it simply don't know the texts. There are "gods" and "teachers" that we can't just spirit away on the grounds that they don't fit into the box marked evolution—because they were here and they left their mark. And that can be shown by anyone who knows the material; the others should take a look! Our stiff-necked belief in evolution has force-fed us—one mouthful at a time—the belief that one thing led to another and we human beings are at the top of the evolutionary pile. That is no more true than the religious claim that we are the pinnacle of creation. The wise academics of our age cling to the principle of "simple possibility," the "most plausible solution." This approach excludes every other way of looking at things. They are trapped in a kind of thought prison, because once the "most plausible solution" has been found, that's an end to it. What's the point of looking any further? When applied to the most fundamental problems, this methodology, even if it has been declared sacrosanct by the scientific community, only brings us half the answer—if that. And one of these null-solutions is the theory of evolution. Evolution is the answer to many things—but not everything.

Plato Sheds Some Light

Plato's dialog *Timaeus*, for example, is not just about Atlantis, but also deals with geometry and the creation of the Earth.[119] After reading through Plato's writings for a few weeks, I found it really hard to understand why Galileo Galilei was made to suffer becuse of his theories on heliocentricity and why he was almost killed by the Inquisition in the 17th century. Everything that Galileo taught was already there to read in Plato: for example, the fact that the Earth is spherical or that it orbits around the sun. Gaius Plinius Secundus (23-79 A.D.), who also must have studied Plato and Euclid, puts it quite plainly:

> There is a great debate between the learned and the vulgar as to whether there are men dispersed over every part of the earth, so that they stand with their feet turned towards each other.... If anyone should ask, why those situated opposite to us do not fall, we directly ask in return, whether those on the opposite side do not wonder that we do not fall.... It is indeed wonderful that it should form a globe, when there is so much flat surface of the sea and of the plains...thus it is never night and day at the same time over the Earth, for the half of the globe turned away from the sun it is night....[120]

Nothing new under the sun! So, did the knowledge in the Book of Enoch come from the ancient Greeks? Not at all, because, even in Plato's time, it was known that the fundamental laws came from the gods. While we rebel against that kind of notion, it was plain, everyday knowledge to the Greek philosophers—these days, we'd call them scientists. Here's an example:

The participants of the *Gorgias* dialog were Socrates, Charephon, Gorgias, Callicles, and Polus—a truly intellectual group. Socrates opened up the discussion by stressing that what he was about to say represented his firm convictions, and he would stand by its truth. Then he explained that the wisdom and importance of geometry had also been known to the gods. In the third volume of Plato's *Laws,* this is made clear. Here the question is asked as to whether there may not exist an inkling of truth in the old legends (even back then!). What is specifically meant are those legends "of former, numerous human catastrophes caused by flooding and similar disasters, from which only a small fraction of the race of man could be saved."[121]

The discussion hearkened upon the fact that mountain dwellers survived who—after only a few generations—lost all trace of memory of earlier civilizations. The people simply believed "what was said of the gods and lived accordingly."[122] To live together in harmony after the flood, "the people had to develop new rules, because no legislator of an earlier age remained."[123] "As we do not make laws for the sons of gods and heroes, like the *legislators of antiquity,* who themselves were the offspring of gods...who *likewise descended from gods,* no one should hold it against us now...." [author's italics].[124]

The most ancient laws were passed down by the gods—and we're back to Enoch and his dictating angels Pravuil and Uriel. "Never!" scream the evolutionists! The Enoch texts were patched together by Jewish priests from the knowledge of the ancient Greeks! Then what is the explanation for the fact that Enoch tells his tale in the first person, telling his son Methuselah that "angels" carried him up to heaven on a fiery chariot and taught him their wisdom?

In Plato's dialogs, *Timaeus* and *Critias* report extensively on the entire story of Atlantis—I'll assume that my readers know how it goes. We hear how *Solon* wrote down the history of Atlantis from an ornamented column, "at the place where the River Nile branches, known as the Saïtic...the great city of Sais...the birthplace of King Amasis...."[125] This wise Solon, who brought the story of Atlantis from Egypt to Athens, lived from around 640 to 560 B.C. Solon copied down the story of an event that happened thousands of years before his own time from where it was inscribed on a tall column. And who founded Atlantis? *Poseidon,* one of these sons of the gods—or, putting it in a more modern context, one of the descendents of Enoch's mutinying crew who had had their evil way with the daughters of men and were not permitted to return and continue their journey with the "Great Glory." Let's not forget: Poseidon also impregnate a beautiful earthly maiden and Atlantis was originally created to provide shelter for his new family. The mere fact that what the god Poseidon created with Atlantis was a superstate beyond the realm of contemporary technological comprehension, populated with a people that were vastly superior to every other race of man, and where the buildings were covered in a special alloy called *orichalcum,* doesn't surprise me at all. But what does this short detour to Atlantis have to do with the Books of Enoch?

Throughout the entire Enoch texts, there is no mention of Atlantis, or of an island that disappeared in a flood, or of a superstate created by one of the "fallen angels." Why not? Because the Enoch texts were written before the flood.

"Only two things are infinite," Einstein once said. "The universe and human stupidity, and I'm not sure about the former." Einstein wasn't insulting any one person; he meant society in general.

Back to Voynich

But isn't this chapter supposed to be about the Voynich manuscript? What has Voynich got to do with Enoch or the finds discovered by Father Crespi in Ecuador? The Crespi collection contains writings engraved in stone and metal that have never been taken seriously, because no one has ever really examined them properly. But panels like the Crespi engravings, the gilded collar with its 16 symbols, or the metal pyramid with the elephants and the band of symbols along the bottom, have all been found thousands of kilometers north of Ecuador, in the United States, and again 12,000 kilometers eastwards, in France. There, in the tiny hamlet of Glozel, farmer Emile

Fradin discovered thousands of pieces between the years 1924 and 1930. These included countless engraved stones and bones with symbols that no one ever analyzed. In his book *Geheimakte Archäologie*,[126] Swiss journalist Luc Bürgin described these articles in detail—without making the slightest impression on the academic community. But they had better take a closer look, because many of the symbols on the *Glozel stones* also appear on the items collected by Father Crespi. Glozel in France and Cuenca in Ecuador are separated by some 12,000 kilometers as the intercontinental crow flies. At least some of the Glozel items have been dated to 15-17,000 years before Christ. So who "copied" whom?

Another enigmatic and highly controversial site is located in a remote valley in Illinois, in the United States. Sometime during the 1980s a number of artifacts started appearing, purportedly found in some cave somewhere by the idiosyncratic eccentric Russell Burrows. Alongside gilded objects, these also include stone relics with engraved symbols. Unfortunately, Russell Burrows has been making a huge song and dance about keeping the location of his find secret. Nevertheless, Luc Bürgin was lucky enough to get to photograph some of the artifacts and thus at least make them available to the public.[127] The symbols on the items from the Burrows cave are suspiciously similar to both those from Glozel *and* those in the Crespi collection. It seems that even in prehistoric times—and long before the flood—there were people who carved similar symbols on stone, bone, and metal. What are we to make of this? Well, we should at least take a closer look and compare these things!

The most impressive piece from the Crespi collection remains the roughly 60-centimeter-tall gilded metal panel with its 56 "stamped" symbols. As Father Crespi assured me—I visited him several times—this was just one prize example from an entire *metal library* that lay in secret hiding places (more about that in the next chapter). Some of the symbols resemble those used in the Voynich manuscript. But that in itself is not reason enough to throw our hands in the air and shout, "Hurrah!" The Voynich manuscript has resisted every attempt at deciphering as did the metal panels in the Crespi collection, even though the Indian Sanskrit specialist, Professor D.K. Kanjilaal, believed he was able to identify certain ancient Brahman characters among the symbols. According to Crespi, Indian priests had assured him that the metal library described the race of man in antediluvian times. That's exactly what Enoch does. And he gets taught the secrets of nature, the solar system, and the universe by "angels."

In the Voynich manuscript, on the other hand, there are hundreds of illustrations of plants that simply do not exist on Earth. With some of them, it's hard to shake off the impression that they are depictions of botany taken down to the very molecular level. And then there are the strange pipes, vats, and bathtubs that are connected to each other and the plants. There are women sitting in them, as though frolicking in some kind of fountain of youth. None of this appears in the Enoch texts. Does that rule out any kind of comparison between Voynich and Enoch?

Enoch is said to have written more than 300 books. Books, in that bygone age, did not mean books as we know them today. They were rather scrolls or—to use a modern equivalent—brochures. Enoch handed these over, don't forget, before his interstellar magical mystery tour, to his son Methuselah to preserve for the generations after the flood. We cannot rule out that one of these "brochures" somehow ended up in an old monastery somewhere and the monks faithfully copied down the indecipherable script. But that's all a little far-fetched. It would just be too extraordinary if the not-yet-discovered Enoch texts included knowledge about alien plants and recipes for immortality elixirs.

A Closer Look at the Text

The Voynich manuscript contains words that are repeated constantly as though they were some kind of key elements.

Folio 76 of the Voynich manuscript. If you look carefully, you can see that some symbols appear again and again. Image courtesy of the Beinecke Library at Yale University.

Just take a look at folio 76 of the Voynich manuscript (you can see the number 76 written in the upper right-hand corner). Now work your way down, one line at a time, preferably using a cover sheet to reveal each successive line. In the middle of the first line you will see a closing syllable—it's a bit small, but you should manage it—that looks rather like a number "89." On the next line, you will find it again on the left, and on the fourth line it crops up five times, including four words in a row! This "89" also often turns up on the end of the same words. On page 76 alone, "syllable 89"—if it is even a syllable—appears something like 64 times. Thirteen of these are on the same word. I always thought that a word's frequency allowed us to draw conclusions about what it might mean. But this rule doesn't seem to apply to the Voynich manuscript. There is one letter, which looks rather like a "4," that appears about 1,300 times on some pages.

German linguist Erhard Landmann claims to have understood the content of the Voynich manuscript. Here's one example: "The leap from our beginnings in space was truly a great one; and it is depicted in the Voynich manuscript. On folio 'f86rs' of the Voynich manuscript, one can see an illustration of the Pleiades and the star Aldebaran. A winding line connects the Pleiades to our solar system, depicted in the form of a sun with a human face...."[128]

Mr. Landmann believes that the Pleiades are the ultimate source of humankind. One thing that is in no doubt is that many ancient races believed that the gods had come to them from the direction of the Pleiades (Maya, Inca, Maori, and so on). However, I cannot say how close Mr. Landmann is to the truth. The Voynich manuscript has many pictures of stars: sometimes they run around the margins, then they turn up in different colors and sizes, at the top of the page or at the bottom, then again in apparent astronomical explanations above zodiacal signs, or they seem to be linked to the naked bathing women in their tubs. There are even a few that really do bear some relationship to stars in the Enoch texts.

Take the illustration in the Voynich manuscript that features the three circular bands of texts, the stars, and the sun at the center. (See page 86.)

A solar chart from the Voynich manuscript. Is this the link to Enoch? Image courtesy of Beinecke Library at Yale University.

Red-blue rays radiate outwards from a central sun (with a face); in between them are unequal groups of stars. Have you counted the red-blue rays? There are 12 of them. If you think of the circle as a clock, then you can recognize "letters" at three o'clock and, opposite, at nine o'clock. They are the same on both sides—although the text at three is upside-down. Obviously, the same idea is being expressed twice. Twelve rays coming from the sun; between them suns, and all of it cut in half.

What was in Enoch? "The luminary the Sun has its rising in the eastern portals of the heaven, and its setting in the western portals of the heaven. And I saw six portals in which the sun rises, and six portals in which the sun sets.... On that day the day is equalized with the night, and becomes of equal length...." (Chapter 72)[129]

Enoch speaks of "twelve portals" subdivided into six. The illustration in the Voynich manuscript shows exactly the same. Well, it could be just a coincidence, but maybe it will help the cryptographers in their long search for a solution, because at least they now have a clue what it's about.

As to the speculation about the origin of the Voynich manuscript, I think two of the options I mentioned can be forgotten straight away. The manuscript did not originate from the pen of any kind of Christian cleric. Why not? There is absolutely no Christian symbology in the entire manuscript—and any Christian pseudo-saint would never have drawn all those bare ladies in their baths or all the plants. That's a naked fact.

And the dreamer from the asylum? Not impossible, but this poor soul would have had to know a lot about astronomy. Look at Enoch's portals in which the sun rises and the equivalent diagram in the Voynich manuscript.

"Man will occasionally stumble over the truth, but most of the time he will pick himself up and continue on."

(Sir Winston Churchill, 1874–1965)

Debunking

the

Debunkers

A Storm of Indignation

My book *Aussaat und Kosmos* (its English title was *The Gold of the Gods*) was published in August 1972. The work was 266 pages of text, and in just 12 of them I described an underground cave system in Ecuador in South America.

I wrote about a table and some chairs that could be found in the tunnels and caverns, continuing thus:

> Behind the chairs you can see animals—saurians, elephants, lions, crocodiles, jaguars, camels, bears, monkeys, bison, wolves—between them creeping lizards, snails, crustaceans. As though they had been cast where they stood, casually and amicably lined up in a row. Not in pairs, like the illustrations of Noah's Ark. Not sorted according to genus and species, like a zoologist might have preferred to have seen it. And not in a hierarchy of natural evolution, like a biologist would want to see. No, it is more like some kind of zoological garden of insanities, and all the animals are made of pure gold....
>
> Opposite this garden of beasts, to the left and behind some kind of conference table, could be seen a library consisting of metal panels. Some of them panels, some of them merely metal foils, just millimeters thick....They stand next to each other like the bound pages of some giant book. Every panel contains writing, stamped and evenly spaced as if written by some kind of machine. Moricz still hasn't managed to count all the pages of this massive metal library, but I accept his estimate that they number in the thousands.
>
> Whoever the creator of the library might have been and regardless of when he might have put it together, it is clear that this great, unknown bibliophile and his helpers were the masters of several different techniques for producing "made-to-measure" metal pages in large quantities. He also knew letters, with which he planned to tell future generations something that was important to him. This metal library was built to last; so that it would remain readable forever....[1]

These short passages from the book were enough to create a worldwide storm of indignation. It started in the German-speaking countries, where most of the major magazines accused me of lying, spread to the United States, and then spread into the Spanish-speaking world. It was noted in every press archive, from where it doubled and quadrupled and became an avalanche that completely steamrolled me. My reputation as an author was completely destroyed. People knew me as a peddler of fairytales and a swindler who was no longer to be believed. Archeologists announced that there *were* no major unexplored cave complexes in Ecuador. The ones that were there had already been examined to the last inch by scientists. And of course, there was no metal library, and the metal panels in Father Crespi's yard were nothing but cheap fakes. I had completely duped my readers with a totally made-up story, just so I could make money.

Naturally, I tried my best, back then, to defend myself—without the slightest success. I was at rock bottom, and today I ask myself how I managed to pull through and publish another 20 successful nonfiction books in many different countries and languages after *The Gold of the Gods* (and a few novels, too!). Okay, I did all right, despite all the trouble, so why bring it all up again here and now? Those who are believed to be dead often live longer! The story of this metal library is about to get hotter than ever. Behind a veil of secrecy, the race to find a certain location in Ecuador has already started. I know the geographic location—and so do a few others! Smart journalists will be following this red-hot and sensational trail and will inevitably trip over the old snippet from *The Gold of the Gods.* And yet again, the archives will be plundered and the old stories about Erich von Däniken and his behavior will resurface. Because no one really knows—or can know—what actually happened 35 years ago.

What on Earth did I do? Where did this story about an underground metal library really come from? Did I really make it all up to make myself sound more important than I really was? What kind of fool must I have been, and why did I write that I was there in person if none of it could possibly have been true?

None of it?

And Now for Some Truth

Decades have passed since *The Gold of the Gods* was published. I have always maintained a meticulously well-organized archive. And now with a 35-year cushion, I finally feel ready to publish certain documents from that time. This is nothing to do with proving that I'm right, or even for my own vanity. It's just an anathema to me to think that such an unbelievable treasure should just disappear forever or—even worse—be appropriated by some religion. I want to show what really happened and what the current situation is regarding this hidden treasure. Who lied? When? Why? What efforts have been made to clarify the situation? And where, for heaven's sake, is this metal library?!

Before I get going, I'd like to clear up a few basic points.

Since 1966—the year my first book, *Chariots of the Gods,* was published—I have written 29 books. In my youth, I was perhaps not as careful as I am now, not self-critical enough and a bit too trusting of some of my information sources. I often accepted information from third parties as being "the real McCoy," got carried along by my own enthusiasm, or made errors in evaluating some kind of evidence. To err is human, as they say, and it doesn't hurt to admit it. In the 9,000 or so pages that I have written it was inevitable that there would be an error or two thrown in, or that over time it turned out that the "other side" was right after all and I was wrong. These days, when I discuss something with an expert, I know from the very start that he knows 10 thousand times more about his specialist subject than I do. These days, it's more about not bluffing, not lying, and certainly not about trying to pull the wool over anyone's eyes. "Listen and don't butt in" has been my philosophy for years now. After every long conversation with a scientist, I can admit that I have learned something new—but so has he (or she), because my discussion partners must practically always admit that they, too, know very little of my specialist knowledge. Mistakes can be corrected or put right.

This conclusion is, in itself, nothing special, because it applies to every author in the world. In every work of nonfiction—and very often in scientific treatises, too—you can find errors if you search hard enough. Time doesn't stand still, and our knowledge changes. Science is a living thing—and thank goodness that it is so, one might add, because looking at things in new ways is the only way to move forward.

Now, there are some people who act as if a proven error in a theory is enough to nullify the whole idea. "If one piece of evidence in your book isn't right," I often hear, "then I have to assume that all the other evidence is false." According to this absurd logic, we would have to throw away practically every schoolbook, teaching book, or scientific book on the planet, because time shows us that many things that were once considered unshakeable truth are now known to be wrong.

There is another class of people who allow themselves to be blinded by superficialities and act like arrogant judges. These people are the ones who constantly cry "exposed!" and "fraud!" They are perpetually indignant and act like they are carrying the troubles of the world on their feeble shoulders. And finally, there are the religious types who, although they do not want to see or hear anything at all, (unlike the famous trio of monkeys) can't stop playing the eternal schoolmaster.

This last category, with whom authors have little joy, are the ones who, despite never having read a book, will pick up on some point from a newspaper review or similar, and concoct their own "exposé"—and without actually ever asking the authors what they meant. How often have I read: "Däniken says..." or "writes..." although I never said or wrote anything of the sort? Well-meaning friends often advise me to sue. But if I started down that road, I'd have to employ my own lawyer and would spend around a third of my time tracking down who said the lies in the first place. The sad consequence of the swindle nightmare culminates with the conclusion: "He never denied anything."

Joachim Ringelnatz once wrote: "Boomerang flew away, didn't come back that day. Hours the patient people stood, waiting for that piece of wood." Well, now the boomerang is coming back, even if it has taken 35 years. So what really did happen in Ecuador?

An Expedition Into the Unknown

In 1970, a Swiss national living in Ecuador sent me a newspaper cutting with a note attached that what it contained would surely be something that would interest me. The page was from the prestigious newspaper *El Telégrafo,* which is published in Guayaquil in Ecuador. The headline announced a "genuine subterranean world in America." The sub-headline went further: "The Moricz 1969 expedition will revolutionize world history."[2] The whole-page article was backed up with black-and-white pictures that not only showed the team entering a cave complex, but also the entrance to a subterranean labyrinth. This entranceway, wider than a barn door, gave the impression that it was some kind of constructed opening with mighty, layered, monolithic crossbeams.

All of the expedition team was listed: Juan Moricz, Gaston Fernández, Dr. Gerardo Peña Matheus, Lilian Icaza, Hernán Fernández, Mario Polit, Pedro Luna, and José Rojas. In addition, there were military expedition members, including a "Capitan" Carlos Guerrero Guerron, as well as the national police representatives Officers Ortiz, Benusia, and Sanchez. At the end, there was a list of diverse helpers, guides, and leaders.

All in all, a pretty large-scale, highly organized expedition into the jungles of Ecuador. What were they looking for? The Argentinean German-language magazine *La Plata Ruf* interviewed the expedition leader Juan Moricz. Here is an extract in which Moricz is speaking:

Really, it's not so much a discovery because we have known of the existence of the Cuevas de los Tayos for a long time. The purpose of the expedition was to photograph, film and document a largely unknown or denied archeological reality.... We also wanted to pave the way for a second, more extensive expedition in which we would find proof that this rediscovered subterranean world was where the fathers of human civilization had lived and worked.... The cave system goes on for thousands of kilometers, stretching far out under our American continent, particularly under the Cordillera massif. The air is clean and the ventilation is perfect, and the temperature remains at a constant 20 degrees centigrade. The entrance is located at an altitude of around 1,000 meters above sea level and roughly 300 meters below the mountain's peak. After entering the cave system through this entrance, the light of the torches and lanterns reveals an overwhelming underground vista. Around 60 to 80 meters wide and between 100 and 120 meters high, it looks like an enormous hall with walls and ceiling made of artistically carved stone blocks and panels. But this is nothing more than the beginning of a colossal roadway.... The section that we have explored is little more than a fraction. We were able to discover numerous corridors, galleries and halls branching off this main avenue, but we have not yet investigated them....[3]

The article goes on to tell about the location of the entrance. From the town of Cuenca in the southeastern corner of Ecuador, they set out with a team of 43 mules and expert local guides towards El Pescado, Tres Copales, La Esperanza, and La Union to a local army base. From there they traveled by canoe to La Puntilla, where the Rio Santiago meets the Rio Coangos. Then came a hard march by foot to the small settlement of Guajare, where they set up their base camp for the expedition.

The story, covered in several newspapers and magazines (many more than I've mentioned here), fascinated me to my very core, and was one that I definitely wanted to find out more about. Everything centered on this expedition leader, Juan Moricz. Who was he? I wrote to the editorial office of *El Telégrafo* in Guayaquil and asked them to tell me more! There was no answer to my letter, nor to my second and third. Were they even getting there? So I tried the telephone—a bit of a trial back then in 1970 because there were no automatic connections to Ecuador. I asked for the chief editor, Jorge Blinkhorn, who had written the article, without success. As nothing at all had been published in Europe about this sensational expedition, I was left with little option: I had to fly there myself!

A Fascinating Meeting

On March 1, 1972, I took an Air France jet to Guayaquil. I found quarters in the Hotel Atahualpa and then made my way straight to the offices of *El Telégrafo*. It took a while, but finally I was standing in front of one of the editors, but he couldn't—or wouldn't—help me. Of course they knew Señor Juan Moricz, but nobody had his address. But what about the lawyer called Peña, who was also mentioned in the article? Surely, he must know how to reach Moricz. They had Peña's address and handed it over.

Señor Dr. Gerardo Peña Matheus greeted me quietly in his large and rather cool office in Guayaquil. I guessed that he was around 30. His well-groomed appearance and objective way of speaking made me feel that he was somebody who could be trusted. Within a short time, he admitted to me that both he and Juan Moricz had read my first two books and had already discussed some of my theories. "Is this story about the expedition and the underground cave system true?" I wanted to know. Señor Peña confirmed it with a nod of his head and went on to tell me how they had only been able to explore two cave entrances in 1969, because Juan Moricz had not trusted their military escorts. What? Yes, repeated Peña; they hadn't really had enough provisions with them and the atmosphere was deteriorating from one moment to the next. Unlike the military men and the police officers, the civilians in the party had been unarmed. If they had really stumbled onto anything valuable, they might have had to fear for their lives in the company of these uniformed men. Peña remained completely objective and showed me an issue of the magazine *Vistazo* from December 1969. It contained a long article about the *Expedición Moricz 1969.* I wanted to know if he trusted Juan Moricz: "Absolutely!"

From his office, Peña called several locations in Ecuador where he thought Juan Moricz might be. After what seemed like an age of trying, he finally got lucky, and he told me he had managed to pass on a message to Moricz, who would call back as soon as possible. I made my way back to my hotel for a long overdue sleep. Guayaquil lies on the Pacific coast, a little below the equator. The air is humid and damp, and in my thoughts I praised the inventor of air conditioning.

On the evening of March 4, 1972, Juan Moricz arrived in town. The tall, well-built man had the air of an aristocrat. His steely blue eyes examined me coldly at first, then classified me as friendly before he reached out his hand. We made our way to the bar and chatted about my books, before wandering off with Dr. Peña to the Hotel Atahualpa's classy, ocean-view restaurant. I found out that Moricz had Hungarian ancestry (his real name was János Móricz), but Argentinean nationality. I didn't press him any further on the issue. I wasn't interested in knowing whether he was a political refugee; I was simply burning to find out more about the underground complex. Moricz was reticent at first, but thawed noticeably during the course of the evening and eventually began telling me one of the most unbelievable stories I have ever heard.

There exists, so Moricz told me, an ancient relationship between the Magyars and Ecuador that is thousands of years old. It can be shown by the countless common word roots belonging to the two peoples, which are equivalent both phonetically as well as in basic meaning. Moricz sketched an impressive list on the napkin. The underground world, he said, was the product of one of mankind's progenitors, the *Táltosok Barlangja,* as he is known in the Hungarian tongue. *Táltos* is the Hungarian term for one of the ancient priest caste, and *barlang* means cave. The Táltosok Barlangja had lived in an underground cave system, protected by a holy bird, the very same "tayo"—or "turul" in Hungarian—after which this tunnel system had been named. My head was soon spinning with this confusing lesson in comparative linguistics all the more, because I don't know any Hungarian and was in no position to judge whether Moricz's claims were true. We spoke then about the ancient legend of Romulus and Remus, the founders of the city of Rome with its seven hills. Moricz assured me that the legend—including the seven hills— could just as easily have been about Quito, the capital of Ecuador.

"And what about the metal library?" I asked. "Does it really exist?"

Moricz nodded earnestly. "Down below, there is an oval table surrounded by chairs. Not chairs as we know them, but more like armchairs whose lower part looks like an 'n.' And on top of that is a 'u.'"

"What are they made of?" I asked, intrigued.

Moricz wrinkled his brow and shrugged his shoulders. "I don't know what the material is," he admitted. "It's neither wood nor metal, but somehow gives the impression that it has been cast." Then he went on to tell me about a kind of zoological garden of metal animals, mostly gold or at least gilded. Practically every kind of animal imaginable was down there, even elephants, although they were unknown in prehistoric South America. And then there were mythological beasts, hybrids, chimera, animals that were half-man/half-beast, and figures that he couldn't even recognize. There were even really small creatures, like spiders and flies, mixed among them. In total, there must have been more than a thousand animals that someone had cast at some time in metal. And the subterranean repository also contained other treasures made of crystal and precious stones, "a real millennia-old treasure trove."

"And the metal library?" I pressed.

Moricz paused again, somewhat longer this time, and stared out of the window into the nocturnal lights of Guayaquil. Then he began to tell me about books and sheets of metal: everywhere, engraved writing that looked as if it had been stamped into the metal. The tomes were made of a yellow metal and were very heavy. He guessed that the weight of a single volume must have been around 30 kilograms. This metal library was distributed through several underground caverns. Altogether, there must have been thousands of pages featuring an unknown and ancient script.

"And why do you believe that this metal library contains the prehistory of mankind? That was what I read in *El Telégrafo.*"

Moricz assured me that some of the pages contained star systems and illustrations, graphical depictions that couldn't possibly be interpreted any other way.

The Mormon Connection

I was dumbfounded. Then I thought of Enoch, who I had been interested in since my time in high school. But why should Enoch texts be made of metal, and how on Earth could they have got to Ecuador from the biblical Arabia? It wasn't exactly on the route for the antediluvian prophet or any of his descendents. Finally, I had an idea! The Mormons! Their ascendents are said to have come from Arabia—at least that is what it says in the Book of Mormon. These Mormon stories could actually have something to do with the metal library in Ecuador. Why?

The founder of the Mormon Church—or, to give it its proper name, the Church of Jesus Christ of Latter-day Saints—Mister Joseph Smith (1805-1844) experienced, according to his own accounts, what can only be described as a strange encounter. He told how an angel named *Moroni* came to him and announced that within a mountain, not far from where he was living, lay a treasure in a stone hiding place. Inside he would find a book printed on golden plates whose engravings contained a complete account of the earlier inhabitants of the American continent and their origins. Next to the gold plates he would find a breastplate to which was affixed two stones, called *Urim* and *Thummim*. By using these stones, he would be able to translate the ancient writings. He would also find a "divine compass." All of these items were to be found in a hill known as Cumorah to the south of Palmyra in Wayne County, New York, not far from the hamlet of Manchester.

Joseph Smith did as he was ordered and somewhere below the peak of the hill he really did find the treasures. How he did it, he describes in his own words:

> ....*under a stone of considerable size, lay the plates, deposited in a stone box. This stone was thick and rounding in the middle on the upper side, and thinner towards the edges, so that the middle part of it was visible above the ground, but the edge all around was covered with earth.*
>
> *Having removed the earth, I obtained a lever, which I got fixed under the edge of the stone, and with a little exertion raised it up. I looked in, and there indeed did I behold the plates, the* Urim *and* Thummim, *and the breastplate, as stated by the messenger. The box in which they lay was formed by laying stones together in some kind of cement. In the bottom of the box were laid two stones crossways of the box, and on these stones lay the plates and the other things with them.*[4]

As Joseph Smith, eager as any treasure-hunter, reached in with both hands to touch the objects he felt a jolt. He tried again—and again received a jarring shock. At the third attempt, he was hit by such a mighty bolt that he lay stunned for several moments on the floor. Immediately, the angel *Moroni,* that mysterious nocturnal messenger, appeared and instructed him to return each year on the same day to this spot. When the time was right, he would receive the holy objects.

Four years later, that day finally came. On September 22, 1827, God's messenger *Moroni* presented Joseph Smith with the inscribed gold plates, the breastplate, and the shimmering translation aids *Urim* and *Thummim.*

Smith described the golden plates as being somewhat thinner than one would usually expect of sheet metal; the individual "pages" were held together with three rings; the book was roughly 15 centimeters wide, 20 centimeters tall, and 15 centimeters thick. He had no problem flicking through the first third of the metal sheets, but the rest were fused together into a single block or "sealed."

Today's Book of Mormon from the Church of Jesus Christ of Latter-day Saints is based on the translations of those mysterious plates. Eleven witnesses confirmed that they had seen the plates, but after the work was completed, the angel *Moroni* removed them to a place of safety, to preserve them for a future generation.

In the Book of Mormon, the 24 plates—they are known as the Books of *Ether* and *Nephi*—tell the story of the people of Jared. The Jaredites are said to have been raised by God at the time of the building of the Tower of Babel. He had led them initially into the wilderness and then over the great ocean to the American coast in small boats that were "tight like unto a dish." The light in the dark vessels was provided by 16 glowing stones, two for each ship, which provided them with illumination for 344 days. They also had a compass whose needle always pointed in the direction that they must travel. Both light and compass came from the same mysterious God who had helped the Jaredites in other situations:

> *And it came to pass that they were many times buried in the depths of the sea, because of the mountainous waves which broke upon them, and also the great and terrible tempests which were caused by the fierceness of the wind. And it came to pass that when they were buried in the deep there was no water that could hurt them, their vessels being tight like unto a dish, and also they were tight like unto the ark of Noah; therefore when they were encompassed about by many waters they did cry unto the Lord, and he did bring them forth again upon the top of the waters.*
> (Ether, verses 6 and 7)[5]

Putting the Pieces Together

But what have the Mormons got to do with the metal library in Ecuador, or even with the Book of Enoch? While Juan Moricz was telling his gripping tale in the restaurant of the Hotel Atahualpa in Guayaquil and I listened, fascinated by his tale, one part of my subconscious mind was constantly making connections with both the Book of Mormon and the Book of Enoch. I had been acquainted with the Book of Mormon since my time in high school (two of my closest friends were Mormons) so I knew that the Jaredites were descendent from one of Jared's brothers and Jared himself was—can you guess?—Enoch's father! In my book *The Gods and Their Grand Design*, I looked at other aspects of this story. So, Juan Moricz's treasures in Ecuador could certainly have something to do with the Mormon's Books of *Ether* and *Nephi*. And the connection to Enoch is not so much of a leap either: the Jaredites in the Book of Mormon are descendents of Enoch. And that's not all. Let's take a look back. In the book of Ether, the Jaredites travel to their new home in eight windowless vessels, each one of them sealed "tight." Practically the same crossing is described in the Babylonian didactic creation epic *Enûma Eliš*. It describes a great flood, but the survivor is not named Noah, but rather *Atra-Hasis*.[6] The fragments of the epic that have survived tell how the god *Enki* gives his chosen survivor, *Atra-Hasis,* exact instructions on how to build his ship. When *Atra-Hasis* complains that he knows nothing of ship construction, the god *Enki* draws him an outline of a ship in the ground and explains it to him. American orientalist Zecharia Sitchin writes:

> Enki spoke of a boat "roofed superficially and underneath hermetically sealed with tar lasts." They must not have deck nor openings, "so that the sun did not see the interior." It had to be a boat "like a boat of the Apsu, a Sulili"; and it is the very term used nowadays in Hebrew (soleleth) to denote a submarine. "Let the boat," Enki said, "be a MA.GUR.GUR"—"a boat that can turn and tumble."[7]

It's no different in the Mormon's Book of *Ether*. Ether makes the same objection as *Atra-Hasis*—namely, I don't know how to build a ship—and the mysterious God gives the same instructions. (In the Bible, Noah also receives instructions on how to build his Ark from "God"—whoever that might have been. And Noah is also one of Enoch's descendents.)

The crux of all these complicated observations is this: Joseph Smith claimed to have received his golden plates from the angel *Moroni* in 1827. At that time, there were no linguists or other specialists who could have translated the Babylonian/Sumerian texts, because they were not discovered until after Smith's death—and that includes the *Epic of Gilgamesh* with its flood stories. So how do we explain the congruencies between the Book of Ether and the other texts that only turned up much later? Were the ancient chroniclers of the *Enûma Eliš* lying when they described how *Atra-Hasis* received instruction from the god *Enki* on how to construct his vessel? Why did Noah and *Utnapishtim* in the Epic of Gilgamesh need the prompting of ominous-sounding gods before they had the idea of building watertight and weather-proof ships to survive? In what kind of magic workshop were the artificial lights and the compass used by the Jaredites hobbled together? And who was capable of manipulating genes or carrying out artificial insemination, like the Book of Enoch (and many others!) mentions?

Surely not the great God of the universe who the religions hold in such high regard. It brings us inexorably back to Enoch's extraterrestrials, the "fallen angels" or "heavenly legions." And what was Enoch destined for? To be a writer, who was the recipient of a few hundred books and who then passed them on to his son Methuselah so he could "deliver them to the generations of the world" after the flood. And where did the original inhabitants of America come from? The "bible" of the Quiché Mayas tells us the answer:

> And thus vanished and went hence Balam-Quitzé, Balam-Acab, Mahucatah and Jaqu-Balam: the first people who came across the sea from the beginnings of the sun. Many ages hence they came and died only at a great age. And they were known as "servants of God"

...and they brought with them over the seas the writings of Tula. These writings they called them in which all their history was written down. [author's italics][8]

Montezuma's Speech

In 1519, while the Spanish conquistadores were encamped before their capital Tenochtitlan (Mexico), the Aztec leader *Montezuma* (1466-1520) gave an impressive speech to his priests and other dignitaries that began like this: "Both you and I know that our forefathers did not come from this land where we live. They came to this place, led by a great prince from far hence."[9]

I already knew some of these stories in 1972 because I had been researching the great histories of mankind since 1959. Sitting there, opposite this expedition leader, Juan Moricz, I somehow learned again how to marvel. He claimed to know all of these crazy stories from personal experience. Could I trust him? His lawyer, Peña, who had known him for many years and who had also accompanied him on the expedition in 1969, trusted Moricz implicitly. I thought again of the Mormons and of Enoch, and told myself: none of it's impossible. These ancient writings exist somewhere on our planet—why not Ecuador? Then I asked Moricz what his future plans were.

He wanted to write a book about his experiences, he told me: a book that would shock the world and the major religions to their cores. This book, he said, would have to be published everywhere at the same time. Here, I expressed some quite-justified doubts. Most publishing houses are normally not really set up to bring out books in different countries and in different languages at the same time. Maybe one of the major houses would be able to manage to publish the book in five different countries on the same day, but never in 20 countries. Moricz did not think much of my pessimism. Maybe I could, I suggested, write something about this fantastic world in my next book—put out a tasty morsel, so to speak, to make the publishing houses sit up and take notice of Juan Moricz. I was also pretty certain that I could rustle up some money in Germany and Switzerland for a second Juan Moricz expedition. The figure I mentioned was $200,000. Of course, it was exciting for me to get the chance to do a kind of sneak preview—but in what form? I still had some gnawing doubts. How could I make Moricz appealing to my critical publisher in Germany as well as my readers? "Is there some kind of document," I asked Moricz, "that relates to your discovery and is utterly incontestable?"

Moricz and Peña exchanged glances and then nodded. They could sense that I still had some doubts. In the meantime, the clock showed that it was well past midnight; an Ecuadorian trio were playing their guitars, roaming from table to table, and singing heartrendingly melancholy love songs. We had already knocked back three bottles of Chilean red wine and had really got going by then. "There is such a document," Moricz stated. "We will show it to you tomorrow."

The next day, Dr. Peña handed over an official-looking document. The first page carried the heading "Escritura" and above it the national coat of arms of Ecuador. The document had been drawn up by a notary, Dr. Gustavo Falconi L., and it was dated July 21, 1969. I published the cover page on page nine of *The Gold of the Gods.* I only revealed a small portion of its explosive contents 35 years ago, but here is the entire and unexpurgated text, translated into English:

1st copy, Register of title
in the year 1969 by the 4th notary of the canton
of Guayaquil, July 21, 1969

Dear Minister of Finance,

I, Juan Moricz, citizen of Argentina by settlement, born in Hungary, passport number 4361689, by my own right and by your mediation with the office of his Excellency, the President of the Republic, do hereby declare that: in the eastern region, in the province of Morona-Santiago, within the boundaries of the Republic of Ecuador, I did discover valuable objects of great cultural and historical value to mankind. These consist of metal panels that were created by human hand and contain a summary of the history of a lost civilization, of which mankind has currently neither inkling nor proofs. I have made this discovery through dint of my own good fortune while I was carrying out investigations in my capacity as a scientist specializing in folkloric, ethnological and linguistic aspects of Ecuadorian tribes. The objects I discovered can be described as follows: 1. Objects of various shapes and sizes made of metal and stone. 2. Metal panels engraved with symbols and ideographic scripts. This is a genuine metal library which contains a summary of the history of mankind; the origin of man on Earth, as well as scientific knowledge about a lost civilization. The fact of this discovery makes me the legal owner of these objects in accordance with Article 665 of the Civil Code. However, because these are items of immeasurable cultural value and I did not discover them on my own land or property, Article 666 of the Civil Code applies. As the land and the caves in which I made the discoveries belong to the state of Ecuador in accordance to Article 55 of the current political constitution, I am required to share my discovery with the aforementioned state. In accordance with the Civil Code, the owners of the land are accorded rights over the discovery. Therefore, in accordance with Article 58 of the constitution I have turned to you. Article 58 states that the artistic and archeological value of a find remains under control of the state. In accordance with Articles 3 and 9 of the Agricultural legislation, it is the task of the Finance Ministry to monitor the laws regarding the property of the state, and to inform the President of the Republic.

As a sign of my honesty and willingness to protect the rights of the state of Ecuador, I am registering my discovery with your Excellency, the President of the Republic. I am doing this to ensure that the Republic of Ecuador is in a position to secure both its own and my rights. I would like to request that you set up an Ecuadorian commission of control. I will show this commission the exact position and location of the caves, as well as the objects within. I reserve the right to show the people nominated by you photographs, films and also original drawings. Furthermore, I would like to state that—in the fulfillment of my rights as the discoverer and owner of this find and in accordance with the law—I will not reveal the exact location of the find until the members of the commission have been appointed. This commission should also contain members that I may be allowed to appoint.

(Signed and sealed by Juan Moricz and the lawyer, Dr. Peña)[10]

A Gentlemen's Agreement

This certificate of ownership knocked me sideways. It meant that we were not talking about the vague hope of seeing a metal library somewhere, but— plain as day—"objects I discovered." Engraved metal panels and ideographic scripts were mentioned: "This is a genuine metal library which contains a summary of the history of mankind." I congratulated Moricz, but felt that I had to add that, despite the seeming clarity of the legal situation, I could not write about something in my next book without at least having seen some small part of it with my own eyes. Moricz said that that was not really possible because we would need to put an entire expedition together just to reach the underground caves. But he *could* show me pictures of the main entrance, and I could make copies if I liked. I was happy, but somehow not entirely satisfied. Filled with enthusiasm after hearing Moricz's story and seeing the notary's document, I was burning to get to the jungle and see for myself. If the cave system was as extensive as Moricz claimed, surely there must be other entrances that one could get to without mounting a major expedition. How about using a helicopter?

Moricz waved the suggestion aside, explaining that there weren't that many helicopters to be had in Ecuador and that the few that were around were in the hands of either the military or the oil companies. Then he made a suggestion; I perked up. He knew of a small offshoot of the cave system. There wasn't much to see, but it might satisfy my curiosity. There was one condition, how- ever: I was not to reveal the location and I was to imply that I had actually been at the main entrance. Why? Moricz insisted that if I were to write in my book that there was another entrance—and what's more, an entrance that was easier to get to—or even disclose the location, then the treasure-hunters would soon be swarming all over the place. He didn't need to tell me what would happen next.

We shook on it. To be honest, I would have even agreed to far stricter conditions. I was so excited about Moricz's discovery and utterly taken in by the calm and considered way he talked about it. On top of that, I had been on the trail of extraterrestrials since my youth and often been mocked or met with pitying smiles. And now, out of the blue, here was a chance to make the public aware of a metal library that—according to Moricz—would support many of my theories. What a find! My last remaining doubts had been simply wiped away by the notary's certificate.

The next day, we set off in a red Toyota off-road vehicle, driving for hours in a southerly direction, up and down mountains, until we reached the city of Cuenca. Moricz filled up the tank, checked the water, oil, and spare gas canister, and then we set off again into the wilderness. For me, Ecuador was a "terra incognita," an unknown country. I didn't have a clue where we were headed. Moricz drove down narrow roads past bushes, giant trees, and Indio huts. He repeatedly stopped the car, turned around, and drove back several kilometers. At some point, we could see a large river meandering below us. Moricz stopped, got out, and looked around before climbing back in, driving around a cultivated field and then setting off yet again in another new direction. Suddenly he cried out, "There it is! Up there!" He pointed diagonally upward, toward a steep rocky crag that was totally overgrown with bushes. We got out of the car and scrambled up a narrow mule path to get to the top. Although there was no visible settlement here, an Indio herdsman and two children suddenly appeared at our sides. They were dressed in black ponchos and were wearing broad-rimmed hats. Moricz spoke to the man; I couldn't understand a word. Abruptly, a sloping cave entrance came into view. Behind it was a deep, dark hole. We squatted down on the stone floor, Moricz laying his high-powered flashlight on the ground between his legs.

He had given me a flashlight before we began our ascent. I made the most of the opportunity, and set up my Nikon camera on a ledge and pressed the delayed-action shutter release. Afterward, we crawled a few meters into the cave. From deep within the dull depths we could hear the rumbling of water. I had left my camera equipment outside, guarded by the herdsman and his children. Apart from a few strange figures and stone sculptures that stood out in the scampering torchlight, there was little to see. Certainly no metal library.

Together with Moricz at the mouth of the cave.

Moricz in front of the same cave (during the earlier expedition).

Back in Guayaquil, Moricz handed over a glossy black-and-white print of the 1969 expedition and granted me express permission to use it in my new book. I flew back to Switzerland shortly thereafter and began writing the first chapter of *The Gold of the Gods—but not the way it later appeared in the printed book.* I'll get back to that later. First, I'd like to present a short "film" of what actually happened.

Back then there was a Swiss periodical called *Sie & Er* (*Her & Him*). It had managed to persuade my publisher in Düsseldorf, Germany, to grant it the right to publish exclusive previews of the new book. Months before the book was even finished, extracts began appearing in *Sie & Er.* But the text no longer had quite the same sober tone as I had originally used. So I hopped on a plane—with a copy of *Sie & Er* in my suitcase—and flew off to Ecuador. I showed Juan Moricz and Dr. Peña the extract in the magazine, including the pictures. Moricz could speak a little German, but not really enough to understand the text. I translated, one line at a time. Moricz found the somewhat-theatrical rendering of my work okay. He said that it was like what they do in shop window displays where the products are presented in a more dramatic light. But everything that appeared concerning the metal library and the other objects was accurate enough. A few months later *The Gold of the Gods* was published—and then the real drama began.

Some Unexpected Edits

But how did my book come to be published in a form different to my original manuscript? Well, it's like this: every publishing house employs copy editors who read the works—especially those by younger or less well-known authors—and correct them, revise them where necessary, and sometimes shorten or fill out passages. One such was Mr. Utz Utermann, who had originally worked in the film industry and, since the war, had reworked several scripts into excellent films. I put great value on his qualities as a person and a writer, and I was able to learn much from him. (In *The Gold of the Gods,* in the credits at the top of the third page, Utz Utermann appears as one of the contributors to the book under his pseudonym from back then, Wilhelm Roggersdorf.) My publisher, Mr. Erwin Barth von Wehrenalp, head of the ECON publishing house in Düsseldorf, got in touch with his editor Utz Utermann to find out how good the Ecuador story was. At the time, I was in Egypt, and Utz Utermann had been commissioned to put together an exciting version of the story for *Sie & Er.* He answered on October 7, 1972, in a letter to Erwin Barth von Wehrenalp. I received a copy. The letter explained how the fateful (for me at least) version came about. Here it is in full:

Dear Mr. von Wehrenalp,

After a hectic few days at the book fair which forced us to make a few explanatory telephone calls, I believe I owe you an explanation, too. Of course, I've had a few worried moments, wondering if I could have done more research on the Ecuador issue.

As you know, I spent some more time with Mr. von Däniken in Bonstetten in May while I was working on the manuscript. On the evening of May 14, Mr. von Däniken played me a tape on which he had dictated the chapter about the caves and the gold. My first reaction was: "That's so fantastic, no one will believe it if we don't offer some sort of documentary proof: photos, documents, etc."

Däniken showed me around 15 black-and-white photos and color slides relating to the subject. These supported ad oculos the text he had dictated. When I pressed him to publish all of the photos, Däniken told me that he had promised Moricz that he would not publish certain photographs. Only the photos that Moricz had specifically released could appear in the book. Despite my dogged insistence, Däniken wouldn't be swayed. "No," he said, "I promised Moricz that I would not publish any photos apart from these. Basta!"

Then he fetched the notary's certificate from July 21, 1969, (as it appears on page 9 of the book) from his papers. The certificate a) confirms Moricz as the discoverer of the caves and b) described the objects discovered within. We put the certificate into the book as a piece of convincing documentary evidence.

Däniken also showed me a full-page article from one of Ecuador's leading newspapers—"El Mercurio"—containing a report on the official inspection of the caves by representatives of the state, military, etc. The report lists the members of the expedition by name. It's hardly creditable that the country's leading newspaper would write about something doesn't even exist anymore.

We looked through all of the documentary evidence that Däniken had collected while in the country, to see what we could actually use. We found a business card belonging to the lawyer, Dr. Peña, who looks after Moricz's interests. I said, "We have to put a copy of this in the book with a note to the effect that any scientists who are interested in serious research should contact Peña to arrange access to the Moricz caves!"

Däniken thought it was a great idea. He was immediately in favor of doing just that—without reservation. "That's it! That's exactly what Moricz and Peña need. They're looking for some serious scientific support and they're hoping that my book will help them to find it."

Anyone who doubts a) that Däniken was in a small part (which is all that is claimed in the book) of the Moricz caves or b) that these caves—which Moricz claims to be man-made constructions—even exist, then they must ask themselves the cardinal question:

If Däniken had any doubts as to the authenticity of his reports, why would he provide his naysayers with the opportunity to debunk his claims by publishing Peña's business card?

Do people think he is so crazy that he would sharpen the knife just so that they could scalp him with it? If he wasn't absolutely certain that his facts were straight then he could simply have written about caves that he had seen but—sworn to secrecy—whose location he couldn't or wasn't permitted to reveal. That would still have made a good read and the jungle is big enough to cover his tracks. One thing his certain: without revealing Peña's address any journalistic research would have been next to impossible.

And this brings me to the weak point in the argument:

Didn't Moricz and Peña suspect what kind of repercussions would come from the publishing of a book by Erich von Däniken? Däniken had a pretty good idea. He enjoys provoking discussion. And for that reason alone, he would **never** back up his stories with such flimsy evidence. He could go the "easy route" and make life much simpler for himself by making statements that people couldn't check. Do they think he's such a fool that he would leave a trail leading to his own destruction?

If Däniken was as unscrupulously sly as some people are trying to claim, then it doesn't make an awful lot of sense for him to provide those checking up on him with a means to destroy his arguments. So, what has happened in Ecuador since Däniken made his two visits? Are Moricz and Peña so filled with consternation about the resonance that is now bringing journalists to their homeland? If—and I see no reason to doubt the facts reported in "Die Stern"—Moricz and Peña really did react as described, what is the reason? Did they—at the end of the day—really want to protect "their" caves from state interference? Do they really, as Däniken has told it, have such a manic fear of hoards of treasure hunters?

Did somebody translate the "Spiegel" article for them, which reported that Däniken has earned 3 million Deutschmarks from his first two books? And maybe said to them "Look! Now he's been to visit you, and he'll be shoveling in the money from your caves as well!" The fact that this might lead the two men to be filled with jealousy and drop Däniken like a hot potato seems to me to be a human enough reaction, even if it's not particularly nice. But in attempting to shed some light onto these dubious events, one has to consider all eventualities.

It becomes all the more curious and incredible when one takes into consideration that Däniken, during his second visit to Moricz and Peña in August, showed the two gentlemen three episodes of the preview version in the Swiss magazine "Sie & Er," which contained the entire caves and gold chapter! And he translated it all for them, too.

On August 14, early in the morning, Mrs. Däniken called me and told me that she had had a call from a man in Cuenca, to tell me that Moricz and Peña were over the moon about the publication!

This statement interests **me** in particular, because I—to make the cave texts a little more colorful and provide the reader with a more lasting impression—added a few "lighting effects" to Däniken's original.

When Däniken got back, I asked him what Moricz had thought about this "artistic license." Däniken said Moricz was totally in favor. He said, "It's like a product in the shop window display that you have to put under the spotlight to make it sell better."

Seeing as Moricz had given his blessing to **my** "lighting effects," I was relieved. I wish that some of these journalistic reports only contained that kind of extra color instead of always twisting the facts.

That only leaves the Cuenca gold belonging to Father Crespi.

Däniken has never claimed that the works in Crespi's possession are anything more than brass and silver panels—only, he never actually wrote it in his book. This fact hasn't cropped up in any of the so-called "exposés" in "Stern" or the TV channel ZDF. They showed some objects, but not those that Däniken photographed and put in his book.

Signed: Utz Utermann, Roggersdorf[11]

A pretty long letter, and one that clarifies quite a bit, but it doesn't release me from my responsibilities as an author (even if the pages that were later so heavily criticized didn't actually come from my pen). So, what really happened? Why the sudden attacks and attempts to make me look ridiculous?

The Press Gets Involved

After *The Gold of the Gods* was published, two South America correspondents from *Der Stern* magazine went to visit Dr. Peña in Guayaquil. According to their research, the whole story about the metal library and my visit to the side entrance to the cave complex was a complete fabrication. In the best journalistic tradition, one of the editors of *Stern* asked for my reaction—before the article went to print. I answered on September 17, 1972:

Dear Mr. Blumenschein.

I would like to request an interview with you, so I can present my side of the facts before my reputation is irreparably damaged by a one-sided and biased presentation of the story. As you know, any later retractions or corrections, as well as any evidence presented at a later date are read and noticed by nobody.

Mr. Haaf [*Stern* editor] carried out a short interview with me on the telephone in which he asserted that Messrs. Moricz and Peña had claimed that I was never in the underground tunnel system and all the pictures of the said tunnel system which appeared in my book *The Gold of the Gods* were taken by Moricz.

The pictures **are** from Moricz, and I really have never been to the locations shown in them. But that claim was never made in *The Gold of the Gods*. And in the photo credits, it states clearly: photos by Juan Moricz. On the other hand, I did have the opportunity to observe a small portion of the subterranean complex through a side entrance which—according to Moricz—is normally under water. Moricz told me, during my last visit to Ecuador in August, that what I had seen was "nothing." It was "derisory." What he meant by "nothing" and "derisory" was only this small portion's relationship to the cave complex as a whole. In that sense, what I saw really was "nothing." But to maintain that I did not visit the side entrance, or that what I wrote in *The Gold of the Gods* was pure fantasy, is inexcusable. I would have to be incredibly stupid to print the address of the very person who could deny everything I claim in my own book! Furthermore, I did not print a single one of my own pictures in *The Gold of the Gods*, although I have several in my possession. Juan Moricz asked me not to make anything public which might reveal the location of the side entrance to people familiar with the area. Finally, I would like to say that this entire speculation as to where I might have been and what I saw there to be utterly ridiculous. The most important question should surely be: **Is it true?** Does this tunnel system really exist? In this respect, it is **Moricz** who must make a definitive statement. It is too late for him to backpedal and claim that the "zoological garden," the table, the chairs and much more (that I have not yet written about) was simply a figment of his imagination. I refer you to the notary's certificate of July 21, 1969, from Dr. Gustavo Falconi, Guayaquil. (Document XVII)

And maybe you should also ask him why he had his photograph taken with me and whether the flashlights we had in our hands were just props.[12]

———

The rest of the letter refers to Father Crespi; I'll get back to him later.

Despite this clarification, the October 1, 1972, issue of *Der Stern* featured a devastating article about me. Moricz and Peña had apparently indignantly denied everything that I had written. I was knocked sideways. Only three weeks earlier, on September 12, 1972, I had received an extremely friendly letter—from Dr. Peña of all people:

I just received your letter of August 21. I wanted to let you know that Messrs. Hero Buss and Perry Kretz from the magazine "Stern" have been to Guayaquil looking for information for an article about your latest book. As ever, we were pleased to welcome them here and show them photographs of the subterranean world.[13]

That was exactly the opposite of what appeared in *Stern.* The magazine had claimed that Moricz and Peña had "opened the two German journalists' eyes about Erich von Däniken." So, what happened to the truth? Did the *Stern* journalists simply make up their story, or was the lawyer, Peña, lying to me? I sent two further letters to Ecuador, but received no answer, which didn't surprise me all that much as the Ecuadorian postal service wasn't especially reliable. As it happened, I had an acquaintance, Ms. Pia Buob, whose job as an airline stewardess took her to Ecuador fairly frequently. I gave her a letter to take to Dr. Peña and asked her to hand it over personally. Ms. Buob proved to be an excellent messenger. She visited Peña in Guayaquil and dropped me a line:

Safely back in Switzerland, I thought I'd write you a quick note about my visit to Dr. Peña in Guayaquil.

I went looking for Dr. Peña immediately after disembarking and gave him the letter that you had asked me to deliver. Dr. Peña was extremely nice to me; he invited me into his house and introduced me to his family. They all wanted to know how you were doing and spoke with great enthusiasm about you and your visits to Guayaquil.

Dr. Peña was, however, horrified to read the *Stern* article that you enclosed with your letter. His very words were: The whole article is a lie. His statements to the "Stern" reporters had been twisted around and quoted out of context. Dr. Peña promised me he would write to you on the subject as soon as Juan Moricz had returned from his trip to the caves. He wanted to speak to Moricz about it first.

Dr. Peña and his family wanted to know when you are going to be returning to Guayaquil. They are looking forward to seeing you again, and they all send their best wishes.[14]

More Denials

After reading this answer, I felt enormously relieved. The world was returning to normal, and it was all just exaggeration by the *Stern* reporters. Wrong! The chaos was just beginning! German-speaking TV channels picked up the subject. The head of ECON, Mr. von Wehrenalp, was invited to take part in a TV debate with noted ethnologist Professor Udo Oberem from Bonn. The scientist vehemently denied that Crespi was in possession of any valuable treasures and that the world had known of the Juan Moricz caves for some time. The ECON chief invited the scientist to take part in a research expedition to Ecuador—of course, with me and others in the party.[15] Just one week later, *Der Stern*—which never published anything to exonerate me—reported that Professor Oberem had rejected the offer to travel to Ecuador. Wrong again! Actually, Oberem had accepted the offer on October 12, 1972.[16]

The extremely conscientious head of the ECON publishing house in Düsseldorf, Erwin Barth von Wehrenalp, would have declared "open season" on me and would have dropped me publicly, if my story in *The Gold of the Gods* had turned out to be a patchwork of lies. Logically, he turned to the Ecuadorian ambassador in Germany, Professor Ramón Eduardo Burneo, and asked for his help in this delicate matter. He wanted the ambassador to identify scientists in Ecuador who could, together with Juan Moricz and me, clarify the situation. The publisher also wrote:

I have been informed that you made certain negative statements regarding the book by Erich von Däniken to the "Kölnischer Rundschau." As we check everything that is reported to us, even rumors, I would be grateful if you could also let me know what the facts of the matter actually are....[17]

The ambassador's answer followed just one week later:

I would like to confirm that I would be prepared to help you with your efforts. In the meantime, I have contacted the relevant authorities in Ecuador and asked them to name someone who might be an appropriate member of this expedition. As soon as I heard back from them, I will let you know.

I would also like to assure you that I have at no time made any statements whatsoever about Mr. von Däniken's book to any publication at all....[18]

So what in heaven's name was going on here? Clearly, journalists were making up negative headlines that kept hitting me like hammer blows and providing my adversaries with ever more ammunition to shoot down my theories. And it was happening right across the world! The articles in Germany had been quickly picked up by the press in the UK and the United States and were being cannibalized to make even more sensational stories. The only problem was none of it was true. But the newspaper editors in far-off lands couldn't know that. Major newspaper and other publications were being quoted and being added to press archives. That's how it works: journalists just dip in and help themselves. After all, you can't expect an American journalist to start researching everything from scratch—especially when it's already been done by someone else. The American says to himself, "Well, the German is sitting right on the source of the story, so he must have better and more extensive information than I could get hold of." The system's called ping-pong. Everyone takes material from their counterparts.

Following the friendly communication I had received from Dr. Peña and the visit by Ms. Buob to Ecuador, I wrote several long and detailed letters to South America and asked for an explanation, such as this one from November 11, 1972, to Dr. Peña and Moricz:

As you already probably know, following my assertion that there is a man-made tunnel system in Ecuador as well as a metal library, I have been torn apart by the European press. During an interview on German television, my publisher at the ECON publishing house in Düsseldorf announced that he would be prepared to finance an expedition to Ecuador to prove the legitimacy of both my claims and your "Escritura."

Professor Udo Oberem, from the department of American Studies at the University of Bonn, and I will fly from Germany to Ecuador. In Ecuador, a museum curator and possibly also a geologist are to join the team. The planned undertaking must take place at the beginning of March 1973.

Unfortunately, none of us has the time to spend several months in the country, which rules out an expedition with mules and porters. Therefore, we feel that the best solution would be to fly to the cave entrance by helicopter. The costs will be paid by the ECON publishing house.

1. Would it be possible for Señor Moricz, and would he be willing, to lead a small expedition on or around March 1, 1973, by helicopter to the main entrance or one of the more interesting side entrances?

2. Is Juan Moricz willing to show us/can he guarantee that the small expedition will get to see some of the man-made cave system? It only needs to be a small part which is indisputably artificial and could not have been formed by natural water erosion or subsidence.

3. Is Señor Moricz willing to take us far enough so that we could see some of the underground treasures—in particular the metal library?

Of course, it goes without saying that we expect Dr. Peña to accompany us on this expedition. This short expedition has only one major aim and that is to ascertain/confirm the existence of the underground cave system and the cultural and historical treasures to be found there. A major expedition, including journalists, is not planned until a later date. For the purposes of verification, it is not absolutely necessary to fly directly to the main entrance, as Señor Moricz also knows of side entrances. He could just as easily take us to one of these, providing that we would still be in a position to confirm that the system is man-made as well as see some of the subterranean treasure.

If Señor Moricz prefers not to take us to one of the side entrances, and would rather fly directly to the main entrance, then it is vital the Señor Moricz lets us know how long we are likely to need to remain underground in order to see at least a part of the metal library. If necessary we will have send out a company of porters in advance, or the helicopter will need to make several trips until the required team and their equipment is all delivered to the main entrance.

The proposed helicopter mission would only possible for both Professor Oberem and myself on or around March 1, 1973. We are therefore relying on a quick and thorough response to the questions posed in this letter. As soon as the Señor Moricz and Dr. Peña have confirmed that we will be allowed to view a part of the underground system and the metal library, we will be in contact regarding the structure and the planning of the trip.

I send my best regards to you both and hope that we will see each other again, at the latest in March 1973.

(Signed: Erich von Däniken)[19]

Waiting in Vain

I waited and waited, sent four copies of the same letter to Ecuador—using different methods and routes each time. But there was no reaction. What could be the reason for this lack of response? To be honest, I would have rather jumped on the next plane to Guayaquil, but my schedule was completely filled with lecture tours for the whole of November and parts of December, too. Even a short visit to Ecuador would take at least five days, there and back, and I didn't have five free days in a row anywhere. Christmas was on the doorstep, with all its family joys and duties. I convinced myself that Peña's answer had been held up in the Christmas post. But Professor Oberem and the others were pressing me. They needed a definitive answer, so they could make plans. So, on December 29, 1972, I sent yet another letter across the ocean to Ecuador:

On November 11, I sent you a long letter regarding plans for a helicopter expedition to visit part of the underground cave system discovered by Juan Moricz. To make sure that it arrived, I sent four photocopies of the letter on different days. In my letter of Nov. 11, I wrote that the ECON publishing house would be willing to take on the costs of such an expedition and the German ethnology professor Udo Oberem would be willing to accompany us.

Now almost two months have gone past and I still haven't heard any response regarding my suggestions and questions. The situation is starting to get difficult for me, if not to say impossible. Not only the expedition members, but also the expedition sponsors—the ECON publishing house—are putting pressure on me...[then comes a section repeating, to a great extent, what was in the previous letter]....Bearing in mind that travel expenses are quite significant, it is impossible for us Europeans to come to Ecuador without any definitive assurance from Señor Moricz.... If I haven't heard anything from you by January 10, 1973, I will try and contact you by telephone.[20]

I spent New Year's Eve 1972 with my family in a wonderful mountain hotel in the Swiss Alps. Many of the guests—some of them genuinely interested, some of them mocking—wanted to know more about the metal library in Ecuador. But I was unable to help them. Even the January 10th deadline that I had set for Peña passed by without any answer. The head of the ECON publishing house suggested that we just pack up our bags and head off to Ecuador, even without any undertaking from Moricz. I was strictly against this idea, giving my reasons as follows:

...the planned trip to Ecuador should and must take place. But the main reason for it is to visit the metal library. So we have to overcome this hurdle put up by Moricz and Peña. Even if our plans are delayed because of these two gentlemen, we should just calmly accept them and not get into a panic. We must inform all interested parties in an objective and considered manner....The fact that Moricz and Peña have still not answered does indeed worry me. Although I can say with some degree of assurance that this silence is no personal affront aimed at me, because Ms. Buob visited Peña **after** the *Stern* report. I'm starting to wonder if other parties have gotten involved in the matter—whoever that may be. Those journalists who attack me and tear me to pieces—**and even the subject**—don't give a damn what we bring back from Ecuador if the **tunnel system and the metal library are not part of it!**[21]

What was important to me was to confirm the most important passages in *The Gold of the Gods*, and that was impossible without Moricz's help. He was the key figure for my rehabilitation in the eyes of the world. Today—even after 36 years—I can write all this and quote old correspondence without the slightest hint of bitterness and with no bad feelings towards those involved. Time heals all wounds, as we know. The reason for my disappointment back then was a very long letter that I finally received from Dr. Peña (which is simply too long to quote here in full), which utterly devastated me. Was I living in some kind of dream world? Or had the others changed sides? Peña wrote:

I received your letters of November 11 and 30, as well as that of December 29. In this respect, I must—as Señor Juan Moricz's lawyer—inform you:....

Señor Moricz and I both believed that you would return to Guayaquil at the earliest possible opportunity, to give us an explanation for the rather colorful and inventive depiction of Señor Moricz's discovery in your book (*The Gold of the Gods*), as well as regarding the publication of certain photographs and information for which you did not have our permission. Indeed, particulars regarding this discovery were given to you on the understanding that you would sponsor a further expedition to the sum of $200,000. This second expedition would then make the details of Moricz discovery available to the whole world....

Contrary to any legal position, you have made use of the material provided to you, although you were told from the very beginning that Señor Moricz wished to retain the express intellectual and authorship rights associated with this discovery, as the certificate signed by all the members of the original expedition—which you have seen—guarantees. I enclose a copy for you....

In this manner, you have usurped the right to publish the results of the aforementioned research. You have also commercially benefited from a discovery and from information that belonged to another without even agreeing a fitting amount in compensation....

By exploiting the commotion and natural human curiosity aroused by the story of Señor Moricz's fantastic discovery, you intend to use your numerous publications to put us under pressure to organize a further expedition, from which you will exclusively benefit. You forget that the plan was to organize an expedition to bring Moricz's discoveries before the eyes of the world, not from a philanthropic desire to show everyone that Mr. Erich von Däniken was right. You have unlawfully aroused the curiosity of your readers for someone else's discovery. Now you want to exploit the situation to prove that your assertions were valid....[22]

Flabbergasted!

This blow totally floored me! For several days, I wandered around as if in a daze. Thank heavens I'm not the sort of type who suffers from depression; March '73 would have been the right month for it! I just didn't know what to think anymore. I had only published a few pages about Juan Moricz's discovery in *The Gold of the Gods,* because he (as well as I) had wanted it that way, and that was so he would find it easier to publish his own book on the subject. He had given me those black-and-white photos for exactly that purpose. They were claiming I had used them without permission. I was being portrayed as a complete scoundrel—the whole way down the line—because I had "commercially benefited" from Moricz's discoveries. Moricz was—so Peña's letter claimed—also horrified about the manner in which I had publicized his discoveries. In fact, I had shown him the previews in *Sie & Er* and translated them word for word. Peña's letter also included a document that I—despite his assertion to the contrary—had never seen before. I knew about the "Escritura" (the notary's certificate), but I'd never seen the following:

The undersigned, all members of the research expedition to the caves discovered by Señor Juan Moricz in Ecuador, undertake not to publish any material or photographs in a journalistic form, by radio or television, or any other explanations relating to the expedition, its incidents, or the valuable objects in the caves, the geographical position of the site, the theories and hypotheses which led to the discovery, or any other particulars relating to the expedition. Any public or official statement to the mass media regarding the success, failure, repercussions, aims, realization and all other aspects of the expedition, may only be made by Señor Juan Moricz, who is explicitly named as the leader of the expedition, and expressly authorized to take legal action against anyone who contravenes this agreement, as well as preventing the publishing of any photographs or statements in breach of this agreement. Only the discoverer, Señor Juan Moricz, has the right to revoke the duties and restrictions described in this document at such a time as he feels is appropriate.

(Signed by hand by all of the members of the "Expedición 1969" on July 23, 1969)[23]

It began to dawn on me that perhaps Moricz was being put under pressure from his expedition buddies, who had all been sworn to secrecy. In light of that, this Däniken from Switzerland didn't fit into the picture at all. He was spoiling everything and earning piles of money (allegedly!) in the process. The reality, however, was quite different.

Why am I raking up this old story now, after all these years? Who cares anymore? *The Gold of the Gods* is no longer on the market; my readers from back then are probably all dead or interested in other things by now. And I have recovered from all the shocks and traumas. So, why dig up this long done and dusted story?

Because the metal library has been extensively viewed and described by another source! And because I now know the exact geographical location of the cave entrance! There are some pretty sensational discoveries right in front of us. The old story is suddenly highly topical again. Before I close the door on all this 35-year-old correspondence, which in itself is a chapter in history, and before I tell you any more about the discovery of the metal library, it might interest you what became of the relationship between Moricz and Peña and myself. I answered Peña's "hammer blow" just one week later (I have a hard shell!):

The expedition that I proposed was purely intended to prove to the world that the metal library and other treasures really did exist and could be found in the Moricz caves. This was always only ever about Juan Moricz and not Erich von Däniken.... It is not about proving that "Erich von Däniken was right," rather it is a question of proving that what Moricz claimed, for instance in the "Escritura," was true.

During my visit to Ecuador last August, I showed you the first editions of the magazine "Sie & Er" and we spoke at length about the ways and means an author must use to present his story. We made comparisons with products in a shop window that must be presented in the right light. Moricz said at the time that the means of presentation was only secondary. I would like to remind you that my books are not scientific treatises and that a writer must be given a little artistic freedom.

In your office, Señor Moricz gave me permission to use the photographs which he had given me. This was indeed the very reason why we went to the photo lab and had copies made. What's more, any sudden secretiveness regarding these pictures is fairly pointless, seeing as they were all published in the Ecuadorian press anyway.

It is indeed true that I made an offer during one of our evening discussions to rustle up some money for a further expedition, so that the world would find out about the fantastic discoveries in Ecuador. This financing would have been provided by the ECON publishing house, and if that hadn't panned out, I would have spoken to some other company. If Señor Moricz thinks he can finance his own expedition then that is his affair, and I'm sure he has his own reasons for doing it that way. But what I do find utterly unfair is to present me as some kind of villain who spilled the beans about secrets that were reserved for Señor Moricz. I was not a member of the Expedición 1969 and not a signatory to the document you sent. What's more, I had never had the slightest inkling that such a document even existed. I would like to thank you for sending me a copy, by the way. Anyway, what the document refers to is not what we spoke about in Ecuador. It was clear to both you and Señor Moricz that I would write about the subterranean tunnel system—that was, after all, the reason for our long meetings.

I would like to ask you, Dr. Peña, to think back to our conversations! You know Moricz's and my position on archeology and on the origin and proliferation of Homo sapiens. You are also aware that Moricz and I both know much more than what we say and write. Do you remember our second dinner meeting? Moricz and I were on exactly the same intellectual wavelength. On some of the subjects we discussed, we only had to nod to each other, because each of us recognized that the other knew exactly what was being talked about. What do you think would have happened if I had published the whole story? I can—especially after our meetings—not understand why you are both suddenly acting as if I had hurt you in some way. Moricz wants "la guerra," or even "norte guerra!" But it was he who wanted to reveal the truth about human prehistory to a larger public. Moricz should perhaps be grateful that people are not just talking about his discoveries, but also about him. I have never claimed any of these discoveries for myself; I have always stressed that it was Moricz's discovery. He has—God knows!— no reason to be angry at me and my publications. If Juan Moricz is really in a position to realize his idea of publishing his planned book simultaneously in 30 languages, then it is in no small way down to the doors I have opened for him. It is only through my publications that the world now knows that a tunnel system exists in Ecuador and that its discoverer knows its secrets.

Dearest Dr. Peña, please accept my warmest regards and pass them on to Señor Moricz.

(Signed: Erich von Däniken)[24]

The Plot Thickens

Back then, from 1972 to 1975, a lot of people in the international press accused me of not defending myself against these substantial accusations. They said I had done nothing to shed any light on the truth, had behaved poorly, and had ducked my responsibilities. In addition to that, some people—intentionally—slammed out headlines claiming I had admitted that I had never been in any caves in Ecuador. Humbug! At the very first press conference, I had made it extremely clear that I had not been to the *main entrance* to Juan Moricz's subterranean world, but I had been in a side tunnel—which was illustrated clearly by the photos. All the facts were thrown out of the window to fabricate copy text such as: "Däniken admitted never actually being in the caves in Ecuador." These twisted articles are still coursing around the press archives and—of course—the Internet, where anyone can write what he or she pleases, even unmitigated lies. It reminds me of a TV host who wanted to restrict his guests to "yes" or "no" answers to questions that he asked. It's about the truth—and that can always be established with a yes or a no. Really? Take the following question and try and answer it correctly with a simple yes or no:

Are you finally going to stop beating up your wife every evening?
Yes or no?

Do you get it? The either-or option often turns out to be a dud. It needs further explanation. That's why I decided—as part of the continuing story of the mysterious metal library—to finally clear up the controversy regarding those few pages in *The Gold of the Gods.* And now I finally have the chance to tell how I actually did try and shed some light on the whole matter.

After my explanatory letter to Peña, I received an answer by return of post demanding money. I was requested to pay "the corresponding percentage of the royalties owed to Señor Moricz," which I owed for income arising from the use of the photographs, research, and so forth. At the same time, I received a letter from a certain Mr. James B. Mobley from the "Media Associates Company," a film production firm in the United States of America, who announced that they would making a film about the subterranean caves in Ecuador and had secured the rights. Señor Moricz had turned down the chance to be directly involved, but his presence would not be

THE CRESPI COLLECTION

Father Carlos Crespi was a monk who did missionary work among the indigenous population in the remote valleys of Ecuador. Crespi received or bought many artifacts from these people. The age and origin of these items, such as this gilded totem (right), is still unknown today.

A close-up of a panel showing a collection of strange beings—surely none of these depict figures here on earth?

Pages in the Voynich manuscript include an illustration of an unidentifiable plant (right) and solar charts (below).

THE VOYNICH
MANUSCRIPT

The Voynich manuscript is a mysterious, undeciphered illustrated book written in the 15th or 16th century. The author and language of the manuscript remain unknown.

One of several highly elaborate astronomical charts in the manuscript.

The yardstick next to this carving gives you an idea of its size.

The Raimondi Stela from Chavín de Huántar. Details shown in drawing to its right.

The strange symbols carved into this stone remain undeciphered.

Below: Another stone carving from Chavín de Huántar showing what appears to be a fire-breathing dragon.

THE NAZCA LINES

Compare the size of the car on the Pan-American Highway to the circular Nazca lines.

Seen from the air, the Nazca lines, or "pistas," resemble run-down landing strips. Could the pista on this "sliced-off mountain" be a possible procession route?

The Nazca lines are geoglyphs located in the Nazca Desert in Peru. They are believed to have been created by the Nazca people between 200 B.C. and 700 A.D. Visible only from the air, the lines form interesting shapes, such as that of a monkey (below) and spider (bottom).

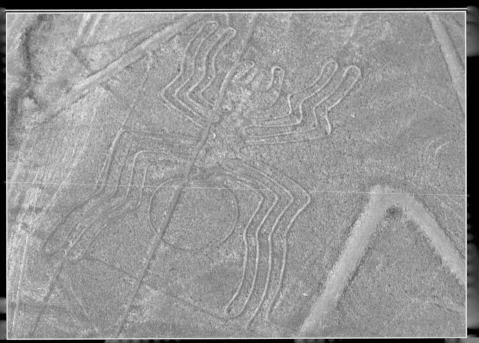

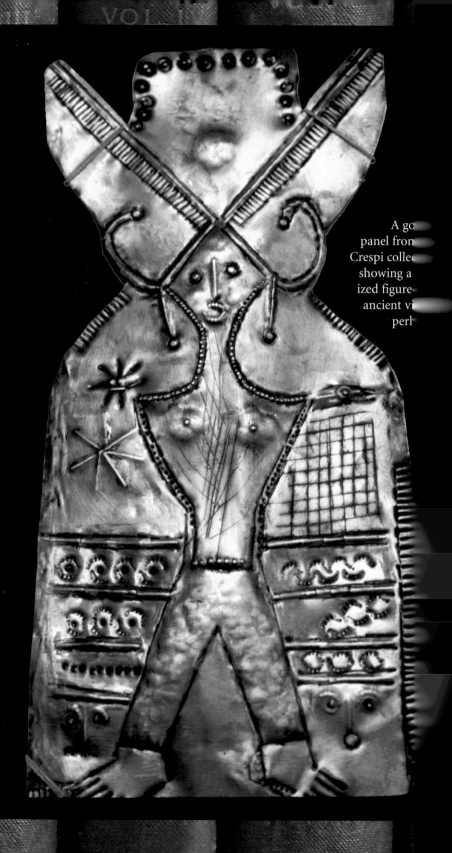

A go
panel from
Crespi colle
showing a
ized figure
ancient vi
perh

necessary as a certain Señor Pino Turrola would be leading the team.[25] To my astonishment I found out that Señor Turrola had explored the caves more extensively than anyone else—and he had done it one and a half years *before* the Moricz expedition! Mr. Mobley assured me in his letter that his film company had drawn up a contract with the Ecuadorian government and registered their rights with The Writers Guild of America. But what electrified me the most was Mobley's claim that the "panels made of strange metals, gold objects, etc." were not found in the Moricz caves; "*rather they were in a chamber many miles away. Its entrance can only be reached by swimming through the river and up into the cave.*"

That was news! If what Mobley said was true, then Moricz had had a notary's certificate drawn up that bore no relation to the truth! It would mean that he had abused the trust of his government and lied through his teeth to his trusting lawyer, Dr. Peña—and me, too! It also meant that the visit to the side entrance was some sort of unfathomable charade. I sent a copy of the letter from the film company to Dr. Peña and also congratulated the film producer, Mr. Mobley, and assured him of my support in his endeavors in marketing the film. In yet another long letter to Dr. Peña of March 16, 1973, I explained my standpoint regarding Moricz's demands (percentage share)[26] but received no answer. Instead, a few months later, a demand for $1 million was delivered to my door. Unbelievable! Someone was suing me for a million bucks for just a few pages in my book *The Gold of the Gods.* Those few pages related to just a small portion of a wonderful story, which was quite possibly made up by the person who was suing me (Juan Moricz) and who hadn't lifted a finger to prove the truth of his tale—even though I had offered to finance his expedition! What the hell kind of world was I living in?

On June 17, 1973, Mr. Ronald Nicholas, president of the *National Leisure Corporation* in Hollywood, told journalist Ron Thompson: "It's unbelievable. The film crew shot more than a thousand photos in the tunnels. They found caverns that were big enough to fit 5,000 to 6,000 people in."[27]

It was all right with me. Whoever turned up with the pictures would only be confirming my story.

Years went by. I challenged and beat Moricz's claim for damages. He himself continued to insist to newspapers and anyone who would listen that the caves and the metal library existed.[28,29] Then, sometime in late fall 1976 (my archive number is missing), the German magazine *Bunte* published a fabulous article about Ecuador. An international team of explorers, led by Scottish cave explorer Stanley Hall, had carried out a major expedition "in the footsteps of Erich von Däniken." Their guest of honor was the first man on the moon, Neil Armstrong. All of the participants were, it claimed, bitterly disappointed with me, as the subterranean caves didn't contain a hint of treasure. I had never heard of any cave explorer called Stanley Hall; Neil Armstrong, on the other hand, was someone everyone knows. I wrote him a letter on February 18, 1977, and asked for more details. A little over a week later, I had a reply. Mr. Armstrong distanced himself from the press statement.[30,31] You can read Neil Armstrong's letter for yourself. (See page 131.)

The Trouble With the Press

Even back then I'd given up asking myself what the hell was the matter with the press. By then, I was well established as a full-blown victim of the system. Just read the letter! I knew, even then, how the media business worked and that journalists simply plundered existing sources to save time; that doesn't make them bad people. So, I was hardly even surprised when one of the major German dailies published an article on October 2, 1982, about a German expedition—yet again "on the Däniken trail"—that had traveled to Ecuador and carried out an investigation of the Tayos caves, easily reaching them without the assistance of dozens of guides and porters, and who also only discovered brass panels and other kitsch in Father Crespi's collection.[32]

University of Cincinnati

Cincinnati, Ohio 45221

February 24, 1977

AIR MAIL

1752

Mr. Erich von Däniken
8906 Bonstetten (Zürich)
Stallikonerstrasse

Dear Mr. Däniken:

Thank you for your letter of 18 February, 1977.

The Los Tayos Expedition, a joint project of the British and
Ecuadorean expedition was formed to conduct a scientific
study of the "caves de Los Tayos". It is my understanding
that the British Army was involved in some 400 such expeditions
in 1976.

Because of my Scottish ancestry, and the fact that the U.K.
side of this project was largely Scottish, I was invited to
act as honorary chairman of the expedition, I accepted.

I visited the exploration site in early August this past
summer. I had not read your books and did not know of any
connection that you might have had with the caves. I made no
statements regarding any hypotheses you may have put forth.

I understand that there have been magazine articles in Germany
and Argentina which reported on the expedition and related it
to your theories. Pictures were included which showed me at
the site. I was not interviewed by representatives of either
publication. I was asked in Ecuador whether I had observed
any evidence of highly developed societies having been in the
area, and I answered that I had not.

I accept no responsibility for anything you may have read in
the European press.

I appreciate your kind invitation to join you in your forth-
coming expedition, but am unable to accept.

Mr. Erich von Däniken
February 24, 1977
Page two

I appreciate the courtesy of your letter.

Sincerely,

Neil A. Armstrong
Professor of Aerospace Engineering &
Applied Mechanics

eem

cc: Stanley Hall
       Maj. C.J.W. Browne

The letter I received from Neil Armstrong in 1977.

But hadn't the "Expedición Moricz 1969" needed a column of porters and even military protection? How did these German "tourists" simply manage to march up to the Tayos caves? The answer is simple: it was 12 years later, and the Ecuadorians had built a road that ran almost the whole way there. The situation in 1982 just couldn't be compared with 1969. And what about Father Crespi? Hadn't it already been established some time ago that all he had in his collection was kitsch and modern junk?

I was already aware back in 1972 that Father Crespi had worked for some time in his earlier life as the curator of the gold museum in Cuenca. So, I hardly think that he wasn't in a position to tell what was gold and what wasn't. The gold museum burned down on July 20, 1962. During my three visits to him in Cuenca, the old man had dragged out metal panels for the camera and said of almost all of them: "Oro...oro...oro." (Gold...gold...gold.) The Father was an old rogue and enjoyed pulling his visitors' legs. During my second visit, he was extremely keen that I take a photo of his latest piece of "gold." I happily did him the favor, although I'm as capable as anybody of recognizing cheap brass. Then he dragged out a rusty old steam iron and told me, with a wink of his eye, that here was proof that the Incas knew how to iron clothes. Extremely shrewd, after earlier visits during which valuable artifacts had been stolen, he guarded his treasures jealously. He hardly let me get near to a single piece; and when I tried to take measurements he would hold up specimens at awkward angles or leant them against the wall. What was I supposed to do? But to accuse the Father—don't forget he was a respected member of the church and a gold expert—of lying would have been too much. I had little choice but to note down his "gold" with a smile. This all the more, because I had been to the gold museums in Lima and Bogotá, and they had had pieces that looked just the same as those in Father Crespi's collection.

So, around 12 years after my visits, a bunch of German tourists wandered into Crespi's backyard. The Father had died a short time before and his successor was all too happy to show the tourists with their fat backpacks all sorts of plunder from Crespi's estate, including a couple of the panels that I had described as "gold." Of course, all the valuable pieces from the collection had long since been removed and were then housed in the Ecuadorian State Archive. Even so, I can hardly imagine that those pieces were just "worthless junk," as the German article had reported. You don't need a vault to store old rubbish. I can well imagine that many of the objects were duplicates: one genuine, one copy. I don't write this just to cover my own back, but from experience, as many of the museums of the world contain imitations of other pieces. Even in the lands of the Andes.

Anyhow, I wasn't in a position to tell what was genuine and what was not, so I wrote in my book *The Gold of the Gods* that the pieces were made of gold, silver, copper, and brass. In my next book, *In Search of Ancient Gods,* which was published just a year later, I was a little more specific: "brass, copper, cheap sheet metal, zinc, stone and wooden pieces...and in amongst all this confusion some real treasures of gold, gold plate, silver and silver plate" (p. 149).[33] The labels underneath the photos were even more cautious: "metal panel" (p. 152), "gold-plated sheet metal" (p. 154), "sculpture" (p. 157), "silver-zinc disc" (p. 158), and "engraved silver sheets" (p. 160).[34]

Practically as soon as he got back, the leader of the German tourist group wrote a book refuting my story in which I was—of course, what else?—again "debunked," "exposed," and "refuted," and we mustn't forget the almost compulsory "indignation" on behalf of the German people.[35] All that was missing were the dancing girls and fairy lights. The book talks as if I had constantly written about nothing but gold, gold, and more gold." in Father Crespi's collection. For a start, it wasn't true. Secondly, my photographic documentary book, *In Search of Ancient Gods,* was conveniently totally ignored. And thirdly, I couldn't know that, between 1969 (Moricz) and 1982, the Ecuadorians had built a drivable road through the jungle that would have made an expensive expedition—as in Moricz's times—completely unnecessary.

The German tourists were quick to point the finger at some of Crespi's panels and "expertly" assess—on the basis of the insufficient weight alone—that they could not be made of gold (Däniken exposed—hurrah!). I already knew back in 1972 that the weight of an object had little to say about its gold content. Professor Gebhardt, director of the Max Planck Institute for Metallurgy in Stuttgart, had told me: "Weight and color say little about the proportion of gold."[36] Professor Gebhardt had been investigating the metallurgical expertise of the Incas for decades and was considered a top expert. A few years later, Professor Heather Lechtmann, head of the Center for Materials Research in Archeology and Ethnology at the Massachusetts Institute of Technology, published an in-depth study on the "fake" Inca gold. The following sentences appear in her report:

> In our laboratory, we analyzed small samples taken from finds. We found that the coating was often only 0.5 to 2 micrometers thick and could hardly be perceived, even at a magnification of 500×.... The lords of the Inca empire used objects that looked like they were made of pure gold or silver.... The methods that the pre-Columbian inhabitants of America used for plating ignoble metals to give them the appearance of precious metals have yet to be duplicated.[37]

And what remains of these so-called "revelations" and the continual cry of "shame!"? Oh, yes! The motifs on Crespi's artifacts.

Archeologists are—at the end of the day—only human and sometimes look the other way, or blurt out premature judgments when objects don't fit into their scheme of things. The Crespi collection is a round peg in a square hole in that respect! It would completely destroy a highly popular preconception of pre-Columbian culture that is perpetuated in countless reference books. The quickest way to write off something like that is to hang the label "forgery" on it. Then nobody has to waste their time looking into it, especially students. I don't doubt that some of Crespi's pieces were indeed modern, but for most of them this couldn't be the case. They were stored up until July 20, 1962, in the gold museum in Cuenca and were classified as genuine and valuable. Then the museum burned down. American archeologist Manson Valentine, an honorary curator of the Museum of Science in Miami and a research fellow at the Bishop Museum in Honolulu, classified *these very artifacts*—the ones that I presented as photographs in *The Gold of the Gods*—as "genuine."[38] And in the previous chapter, I showed you Crespi panels engraved with symbols that can also be seen thousands of miles from Ecuador. They'll expect me to believe next that the Indios visited the little museum in Glozel (in France) before they got to work with their hammers and metal.

I've got nothing against reasonable criticism, even when it sometimes goes against the grain. I myself am a member of numerous national and international writers' associations. I know countless journalists—my daughter is one of them—and have no problem sitting together with them to discuss the pros and cons of a particular situation. I am happy to laugh around and philosophize with my colleagues from the writing guilds. But I *do* have something against this constantly offended and indignant minority, which only takes the trouble to understand the absolute minimum of a life's work necessary to be able to pass judgment on the rest of the things that they can't actually be bothered to look into.

An Honorable Scotsman

Now where is that metal library?

The Gold of the Gods was published in Spanish with the title *El Oro de los Dioses* in 1974 and unleashed a storm of controversy concerning the Tayos caves. (Just as a matter of interest: neither the English title, *The Gold of the Gods,* or the Spanish title, *El Oro de los Dioses,* came from me. Foreign titles were always thought up by the publishing houses.) Anyway, the book inspired other expeditions on the trail of these contentious caves. Newspapers wrote reports about them,[39] and the subterranean cave system was described, at least partially.[40] One of those who had been inspired by the tale told in my book was Mr. Stanley Hall. In 1994, I was in Quito to give a lecture organized by the Swiss embassy and Germany's Goethe Institute.

The next day I met up with Stan, as he calls himself, at his house. My former, longtime secretary and friend Willy Dünnenberger, who has lived in Quito for many years now, had organized the meeting. Stan, as I found out, was of Scottish descent. I knew his name from the newspaper: it was he who had gotten the Neil Armstrong expedition of 1976 off the ground. That expedition, he told me, had only lasted a single day, as the entire team—including the first man on the moon, Neil Armstrong—had been flown directly to the cave by helicopter. Stan had known Juan Moricz for years, and of course his lawyer, Gerardo Peña. I told Stan my side of the tale, without referring to any documents of any kind, and Stan told me he was still hot on the trail of the metal library; the story was too fantastic to be allowed to get lost in the mists of time. I thought much of Stan, both as a person whose word you could rely on, and as a highly competent explorer. And I really believed that, if anyone could find anything here in Ecuador, it would be him—all the more because he had a great reputation there and was also married to an Ecuadorian.

During our conversation, Stan told me that he knew the geographical position of the metal library. It was not to be found in the Tayos Caves, he said. But it was too early to go public with the information.

Stanley Hall had doggedly remained on the trail for all these years and *knew the exact position of the entrance to the metal library.* He made no secret of it and—before his untimely death in 2008—published the mouthwatering and, in parts, painstaking tale in his book *Tayos Gold: The Archives of Atlantis*[41] (in which I appear almost as a kind of adoptive uncle). Hall met up with the only eyewitness who had seen the metal library and the other fantastic objects with his own eyes: Señor Lucio Petronio Jaramillo Abarca. Petronio Jaramillo had been led into the phenomenal subterranean caves long before Juan Moricz by an Indio of the Shuar tribe (previously known as the "Jívaros," a tribe that had been somewhat infamous for its practice of making shrunken heads from slain enemies). Due to severe erosion, the men were forced to make their entry by diving into a river and swimming up into one of the caves, where they spent the whole day and the following night examining the treasure. Stan's story of what he saw can be read from page 185 onward in his book. For reasons of copyright, but also out of respect to Stan's many years of research, I cannot simply quote these simply Earth-shattering revelations here. But I can say that Petronio talked of "thousands of animal carvings," of chimeras, of "crystal-like columns of various colors," and finally of a metal library of many thousands of pages in which each "metal panel [was] around 40×20 centimeters large."[42] What Juan Moricz had told me that night in Guayaquil, a few extracts of which I have given you here in this book, is a mere trifle compared to the description by the eyewitness Petronio Jaramillo.

This subterranean world will provide us with revelations that will be a kick in the teeth for some, but for others an enlightenment. But before that can happen, our so-called zeitgeist has to permit the metal library to come to light. It has to allow research at a level that is only possible in scientific circles. But which science? Conservative archeology, ethnology, and old-school theology? In addition to that, any group would need government assistance to carry out an extensive, large-scale expedition. Will they block it, maybe let themselves be bribed? Will they attempt to tell us—totally objective and deadly serious as ever—that Stan Hall's revelations and Petronio Jaramillo's stories were just pure fantasy? I'm no big fan of conspiracy theories, but I know of two definite cases where this is exactly what has happened: the "Qumran Scrolls" found near the Dead Sea and the hidden chambers under the Great Pyramid. To prevent any possible cover-up or secret exploitation of the caves, Stan Hall decided to reveal the exact position of the metal library. (Hello, Google Earth! Turn your satellite eye toward "1° 56' 00" South, "77° 47' 34" West!). But why is the eyewitness to this phenomenal treasure not all over our television screens?

Petronio Jaramillo was gunned down in front of his own house in May 1998. He left behind a 14-year-old son, Mario.

Stan Hall and Mario attempted to reach the entrance to the subterranean treasure chambers together, but, due to further erosion and other problems that Stan described in his book, the team had to give up the effort just a short way before reaching their goal. If you believe the Internet, others have tried, too. Journalist Alex Chionetti claimed that he was prevented from reaching his goal by the Shuar tribesmen.[43]

And what about Señor Pino Turolla, who allegedly visited the caves one and a half years *before* Juan Moricz *and* had a film team with him? What happened to the film producer, James B. Mobley? Where are the thousands of photos that have supposedly been shot down in this subterranean world? Stan Hall described Pino Turolla as a count of Italian origin who was searching for some proof of extraterrestrial life. Heaven knows who he was working for. And whether he actually ever found anything to support his theories in the Tayos Caves, I cannot tell you. I met Mobley years later in Los Angeles, and asked him about his film and all the photos from the caves. He was friendly but tight-lipped, and said the film would never see the light of day, and neither would the photos. "Why on Earth not?" I wanted to know, "Your company invested some hard bucks in that project." He smiled smugly and explained somewhat ambiguously that his company had got back a lot more money than it had invested. "From whom? For heaven's sake! I just don't believe this!" Mobley held his tongue, thanked me for the drink, and left.

It's meetings like this that really make me mad, without even getting onto the subject of global conspiracies. And what about Juan Moricz? Surely, at least he must have some interest in proving his story and blazoning it out to the world.

Juan died on February 27, 1991, a short time before his 69th birthday. He had again discovered gold and never missed any opportunity to insist his story was true. How can that be? After it had been conclusively proven that the metal library wasn't located in the Tayos Caves? The actual entrance lay around 100 kilometers away from the Tayos Cave. What should I think of Moricz's claims now? I have never judged him and remained, despite the problems that we had with each other, of the opinion that he was a great man. He knew a huge amount—especially in my specialty area—was well read, and always behaved like a gentleman. With the benefit of hindsight, I can even understand why he reacted so angrily to my actions, especially after he was put under increasing pressure following the publication of my book (he had similar problems with Stan Hall, and for the same reasons). Today, I believe that Juan Moricz's caves most probably did contain treasure. These were—*after* the publication of *The Gold of the Gods* and *because* of the risk of treasure hunters—removed and put somewhere else. It cannot, however, be the same material that Petronio Jaramillo saw and described, as that unique sighting took place *before* 1964. And the lawyer, Dr. Peña? A noble and highly intelligent gentleman, thorough and neat, who did nothing more than represent the interests of his client, Juan Moricz. How much of Moricz's story he himself believed, I cannot say.

A Twist in the Tale

The explosive story of the metal library is only just beginning, thanks to Stanley Hall! From his book and further conversations I had with him (he visited me in Switzerland), I found out that a small expedition of Mormons had already visited the caves in 1968—one year before the Moricz expedition! Now's the time to prick up your ears! Let's take a look back: the Mormons are descended from the Jaredites. Jared was Enoch's father. He, you will remember, wrote down books that were dictated to him by extraterrestrials and handed them down to his sons to be preserved for future generations. Led by a "god," the Jaredites reached the South American coast after 344 days in eight windowless boats. The Mormon books of *Ether* and *Levi* describe this in detail. What do these ancestors of today's Mormons—or the descendents of Jared—have to do with the writings on the metal panels? A few quotes from the Book of Mormon reveal that it was exactly this type of metal panel that they carried. Before the journey over the great ocean, the panels had to be secured: (Words and numbers in parentheses indicate the book and chapter in the Book of Mormon.)

> *(Nephi 3:3) For behold, Laban hath the record of the Jews and also a genealogy of my forefathers, and they are engraven upon plates of brass. (3:4) Wherefore, the Lord hath commanded me that thou and thy brothers should go unto the house of Laban, and seek the records.... (3:24) And it came to pass that we went in unto Laban, and desired him that he would give unto us the records which were engraven upon the plates of brass, for which we would give unto him our gold, and our silver, and all our precious things. (4:16) And I also knew that the law was engraven upon the plates of brass. (4:17) And again, I knew that the Lord had delivered Laban into my hands for this cause—that I might obtain the records according to his commandments. (5:10) And after they had given thanks unto the God of Israel, my father, Lehi, took the records which were engraven upon the plates of brass, and he did search them from the beginning. (5:11) And he beheld that they did contain the five books of Moses, which gave an account of the creation of the world, and also of Adam and Eve, who were our first parents. (5:18)...that these plates of brass should go forth unto all nations, kindreds, tongues, and people who were of his seed. (5:19) Wherefore, he said that these plates of brass should never perish; neither should they be dimmed any more by time.... (5:22) Wherefore, it was wisdom in the Lord that we should carry them with us, as we journeyed in the wilderness towards the land of promise.*[44]

The book tells of "brass plates," although we should perhaps not take the word *brass* too literally. After all, these plates were intended to survive for millennia (and not *be dimmed any more by time*). The word *brass* may have come about simply as a result of the translation or to protect the real truth. If the translator had, for example, used the word *gold,* then the desirability of these plates would have been increased manifold. And anyway, only a microcoating of gold would have been necessary. Think back to the phenomenal metal-processing techniques of the pre-Columbian Incan tribes who, after all, must have learned their skills from somewhere or someone. Anyhow, these brass plates contained accounts "*of the creation of the world, and also of Adam and Eve, who were our first parents.*" And they were to be distributed "*unto all nations, kindreds, tongues, and people.*" Obediently, the Jaredites dragged these important chronicles with them across the sea to America. And once in America, the number of plates increased as ever new accounts were added:

> (*Nephi 9:4*) *Upon the <u>other</u> plates should be engraven an account of the reign of the kings, and the wars and contentions of my people.... (9:5) <u>Wherefore, the Lord hath commanded me to make these plates for a wise purpose in him, which purpose I know not.</u>* [author's underlining][45]

So, new plates were constantly being added to the old ones and—as the second book of *Nephi* describes, from Chapter 13 onward—copies were also being made of both old and new plates using "ore." The collection grew and because Nephi's descendents also wrote their history on metal plates, the metal library of the ascendents of today's Mormons must have consisted of thousands upon thousands of plates.

A Fantastic Voyage

Petronio Jaramillo, the murdered eyewitness to the subterranean treasures, told not only of engraved panels, but also of inexplicable things such as, according to Hall's *Tayos Gold*, "crystal-like columns of various colors." He also mentioned a kind of artificial light and colored stones, as well as mysterious walls that were "crystal in appearance." Pomposity? Now, hold on a minute!

The Jaredites crossed the ocean in eight ships. But what were these vessels actually made of?

(1 Nephi, 18:2) Now I, Nephi, did not work the timbers after the manner which was learned by men, neither did I build the ship after the manner of men; but I did build it after the manner which the Lord had shown unto me; wherefore, it was not after the manner of men. [author's underlining][46]

Boats that are not made using human methods—in other words, "terrestrial" methods—can only have been made using extraterrestrial methods. These would most probably have included new materials, joins, alloys, and tools that men did not know at that time. But the ETs did! Petronio Jaramillo saw these kinds of alloys and compared them crystal and quartz. It can hardly have been phantom ships, as I'm sure some clever psychologists will attempt to argue. The boats were completely watertight and totally storm-resistant. And where did the artificial light and the other things that Petronio described come from?

(1 Nephi 16:10) And it came to pass that as my father arose in the morning, and went forth to the tent door, to his great astonishment he beheld upon the ground a round ball of curious workmanship; and it was of fine brass. And within the ball were two spindles; and the one pointed the way whither we should go into the wilderness.... (16:16) And we did follow the directions of the ball, which led us in the more fertile parts of the wilderness.[47]

This curious ball seems to be more than just a compass. It also carries out other vital functions.

(1 Nephi 16:26) And it came to pass that the voice of the Lord said unto him: Look upon the ball, and behold the things which are written. (16:27) And it came to pass that when my father beheld the things which were written upon the ball, he did fear and tremble exceedingly....[48]

A flying, speaking, and picture-producing ball. How come the "Lord" didn't make it all a little bit simpler? Wasn't he capable? All these mysterious objects—compass, speaking ball with integrated holographic functions—helped the Jaredites in their journey across the ocean. And the artificial light that Petronio Jaramillo claimed to have seen?

After the Jaredites had built their unique vessels with the help of their "Lord," they realized that it was going to be pitch black inside them:

> *(Ether 2:18) And it came to pass that the brother of Jared cried unto the Lord, saying: O Lord, I have performed the work which thou hast commanded me, and I have made the barges according as thou hast directed me. (2:19) And behold, O Lord, in them there is no light; whither shall we steer? And also we shall perish, for in them we cannot breathe, save it is the air which is in them....* [49]

Simple problems like this were easy for the "Lord" to solve. He created shining stones (see Ether 6:2), 16 of them in all, and gave them to the Jaredites.

> *(Ether 6:3) And thus the Lord caused stones to shine in darkness, to give light unto men, women, and children, that they might not cross the great waters in darkness.* [50]

To make sure that his people had fresh air to breathe, he had them drill special holes that would let in air but kept out water. Today, we called them nonreturn valves. Technically flawless. There is even an explanation for the luminous stones. Certain chemicals, when brought into contact with oxygen, begin to glow. In the subterranean rooms visited by Petronio Jaramillo the air was admittedly damp but nonetheless pleasant. In other words, there was enough oxygen to sustain a long-term chemical reaction. The "stones of the Lord" are still working thousands of years later. Petronio Jaramillo didn't make it up.

It all seems a bit much, all these things we are suddenly being confronted with. But there is a certain logic behind it all. I would like to help to encircle all these mysterious facts and expand on them by applying today's standard of knowledge. The consequences of this will be compelling—and uncanny at the same time.

In the book *Ether* in the Book of Mormon, Jared's brother reveals that he has been ordered to hide the engraved plates again (Ether 4:3), and he continues:

> *(Ether 4:4) Behold, I have written upon these plates the very things which the brother of Jared saw; and there never were greater things made manifest than those which were made manifest unto the brother of Jared. (4:5) Wherefore the Lord hath commanded me to write them; and I have written them. And he commanded me that I should seal them up; and he also hath commanded that I should seal up the interpretation thereof....*[51]

This revelation by Ether (which is why it is known as the Book of Ether) is not referring to those metal plates that were first written in the Americas, but expressly to the original plates:

> *(Ether 1:3) ...the first part of this record, which speaks concerning the creation of the world, and also of Adam, and an account from that time even to the great tower, and whatsoever things transpired among the children of men until that time, is had among the Jews. (1:4) Therefore I do <u>not</u> write those things which transpired from the days of Adam until that time; <u>but they are had upon the plates; and whoso findeth them, the same will have power that he may get the full account.</u>* [author's underlining][52]

The plates are to be hidden—and are consequently dutifully concealed. By whom? By Moroni, a person who lives long after the Jaredites. He tells us this in person: "I am the son of Mormon..." (Mormon 8:13).[53] And what does he do?

> *(Mormon 8:14) And I am the same who hideth up this record unto the Lord; the plates thereof are of no worth, because of the commandment of the Lord. For he truly saith that no one shall have them to get gain; but the record thereof is of great worth; and whoso shall bring it to light, him will the Lord bless.*[54]

The circles get smaller; the conclusions more convincing. But we are still lacking the last drop of color to transform this portrait into a grand master.

It is *Moroni* who closes the loop. Following the instructions of his "Lord," he tells us that the treasure will come "out of the earth." And as the icing on the cake, he even tells us approximately when.

> *(Mormon 8:16) And blessed be he that shall bring this thing to light; for it shall be brought out of darkness unto light, according to the word of God; yea, it shall be brought out of the earth, and it shall shine forth out of darkness, and come unto the knowledge of the people.... (8:26)...and none can stay it; and it shall come in a day when it shall be said that miracles are done away; and it shall come even as if one should speak from the dead. (8:29) Yea, it shall come in a day when there shall be heard of fires, and tempests, and vapors of smoke in foreign lands; (8:30) And there shall also be heard of wars, rumors of wars, and earthquakes in divers places.*[55]

Let me recapitulate:

- ► Two extraterrestrials ("the like of which I never saw on earth") disinfect Enoch with a wonderfully smelling paste and dress him in new clothing.

- ► They bring him to a mother ship.

- ► He learns to write and is given "a reed of quick-writing." Many books are dictated to him.

- ► Before he finally leaves the Earth, he passes on these books to his brother and sons "for the generations after the flood."

- ► Enoch's books are hidden. Possibly some of them are in the Great Pyramid; others make their way to Laban, who is somewhere near Jerusalem.

- ► One of Enoch's brothers is given the task—by an unidentified "God"—of retrieving metal panels from Laban.

- ► This group calls themselves the Jaredites—the descendents of Jared, Enoch's father.

- The "Lord" helps them to create phenomenal ships "not after the manner of men," hands over a mysterious ball that can talk and produces holographic pictures, as well as 16 "shining stones."

- The Jaredites reach America, along with their ancient scriptures on metal panels, and start creating new plates to record their history in America. The old plates are probably duplicated here.

- Joseph Smith receives an order to translate these plates. (I will attempt to show how this may have been possible later.) The result is the Book of Mormon, the "bible" of the Church of Jesus Christ of Latter-day Saints.

- This book tells us that the metal library is safely hidden, but will come to light when it can be said that "miracles are done away" (that is, they have ceased). It will also be a time of "fires, and tempests, and vapors of smoke in foreign lands" and "wars, rumors of wars, and earthquakes in divers places."

- The writings on the metal plates will come to the people "even as if one should speak from the dead" (in other words, as if the dead were telling their story).

- A metal library is discovered in Ecuador, complete with artificial light and other wonders.

- The eyewitness Petronio Jaramillo describes the details of the fantastic subterranean cave system, including a library made of metal.

- A small group of modern Mormons visit the Tayos Caves in Ecuador in 1968 in the hope of discovering the legacy of their forefathers, the Jaredites.

Strange, to say the least. Joseph Smith, the founder of the Mormon faith, could not have known—back in 1827—anything about a subterranean metal library in Ecuador, and certainly nothing about the Babylonian creation epic *Enûma Eliš,* in which the same shipbuilding story is described as in the Book of Ether.

So, Who Is God?

The reality is more fantastic than the fantasy. Once again—like in the earlier books—we are forced to ask the question, who is or were the god or gods that moved among us all those millennia ago? As a religious man who still prays daily, my faith begins with the creation of the universe. *My* idea of God is of an eternal, omnipresent, timeless, and almighty being who would never feel the need to cruise around Earth in any kind of vehicle that throws up sand, makes a lot of noise, radiates blazing light, and, what's more, is extremely dangerous to any human in the vicinity (see Genesis or the prophet Ezekiel in the Old Testament). I know intelligent works by philosophers and theologians on "God, the being," but none of them have created a satisfactory definition of God. (If anybody is interested in my theories about what God is, refer to my book *The Gods Were Astronauts.*)

Independently of the "Great Spirit of Creation," as I describe God, certain beings were clearly active on Earth many thousands of years ago and mankind believed them to be gods. The psychological explanation that our "simple" forefathers had mistaken mighty forces of nature for divine visitations falls apart at the latest when these gods start speaking, giving instructions, or imparting astronomical or technical knowledge that those millennia-old human societies could not have had a clue. Or was it simply a force of nature that handed over the "a reed of quick-writing"? Then disinfected him, dressed him, and transported him in a fiery chariot into the clouds? And *then* dictated to him information on the phases of the moon and the paths of the sun? Was it the storm, the silent stars in the firmament, the blinding lightning from the black clouds that taught our ancestors—who themselves had only just come down from the trees—how to write? And who was this idiosyncratic god followed by the Jaredites with their metal plates?

If the Great Spirit of Creation had wanted to relocate a group of people to a distant continent—what we now know as America—then why would he need to bother with the tedious process of building eight tiny ships? Wouldn't the almighty God of humankind have been able to simply spirit them there with a wave of his hand or a mere thought? Or—as it is written in Sura 2, verse 117 of the holy Qur'an—"when He wills a thing to be, He but says unto it, 'Be'—and it is." Did the "Lord" of the Jaredites really have no divine powers? The fact that he shipped the Jaredites and their metal library across the ocean in those small, handmade vessels seems to indicate this. Why did the "Lord" need to provide technical instructions on how to construct the boats? And did he simply forget about the need for lighting and ventilation, so that he needed to be reminded about it by the humans? Even if the god of the Jaredites simply didn't feel like performing wonders; even when he specifically wanted his people to work hard for their own redemption, it remains incomprehensible why he didn't provide plans for a more significant vessel, such as Noah's Ark. And if it had to be ships like watertight nutshells, couldn't the eternal god of winds and clouds have at least managed to conjure up some calm seas for his travelers? It is all rather vexing and full of contradictions. Was the god of the Jaredites deliberately trying to provoke the question: why technology and not miracle? Why this dangerous journey over stormy waters? Would the "Lord" have been able to intervene if his people had really gotten into trouble?

The contradiction between the concept of the Great Spirit of Creation (= God) and the deified figures of ancient writings is clear. My small intellect drives me to search for these gods of antiquity, because they were clearly here and they left a significant mark. The conclusion for anyone knowledgeable in the field—and here I include myself after my 50 years of research and 30 books on the subject—is absolutely certain. If you bore for long enough, you leave a hole. Apparent answers, half-truths, and the lies from the literature simply won't do anymore. Curiosity is an untamable beast that, even on its deathbed, is still looking for the next answer. It asks and asks and asks: How was it back then? Why did that happen? Who were these gods that so impressed early man that world religions arose from it? One thing can be said for sure: the gods of the major religions didn't appear in fairy costumes and conjure people from one place to another with their magic wands. Admittedly, the ancient gods did seem to fly around the place, from one country to another, and occasionally—the individual cases are documented—even took human passengers. However, they never took entire peoples in their flying monstrosities. But this is all technology, not miracles. Why? Did these so-called gods not have any access to the phenomenal possibilities available to the Great Spirit of Creation? Or are all these holy books, including the Book of Mormon, simply fabrications?

The Vatican recently announced that the Roman-Catholic Church is the only true church of Jesus Christ, and the Protestant and Evangelical churches "are not churches in the true sense"[56] (statements like this crop up on a regular basis—every few decades or so). On the *Dienstags Club* (*Tuesday Club*), a program on Swiss TV, I recently watched a debate between Catholic and Evangelical theologians. The Catholic, clearly highly schooled in theological matters, explained how the statements made by the Roman-Catholic congregation were to be understood, and the Protestant clergyman defended ecumenism and insisted that all Christian communities lived according to the same gospel and the teachings of Jesus Christ, the founder of Christianity. Heavens above! Do they not know, or do they simply not want to know, anything about the "urtexts" and the millennia-old deception of these gospels?

Is it the same story with the chronicles of *Ether* and *Levi* in the Book of Mormon? Are these metal plates, which were supposedly written thousands of years ago, simply a figment of someone's imagination? A holy lie? Who is this Joseph Smith anyway? And how did he discover and translate the plates?

Joseph Smith

Among the hordes that made their way to the New World during the great waves of immigration that took place 180 years ago was a Scottish family with eight children that settled in Palmyra in New York State. The area that the Smiths settled in was right on the edge of civilization, where they faced a hard daily struggle just to get by. The new arrivals from Europe were a hardworking bunch: they brought not only tools and an impressive work ethic with them, but also numerous religious views, which they attempted to spread with missionary fervor. New sects and religious groups sprang up everywhere. Apostles of salvation from countless faiths preached on street corners, overtrumped each other with the boldest of promises during battles of words, and often attempted to capture the souls of believers with grim threats from beyond. Chapels, temples, and churches shot out of the ground like mushrooms, just as if the devil himself had just arrived in town to confuse the spirits of the settlers. Mother Smith and three of her children joined the Presbyterians. Son Joseph, now 18 years old, had his problems, however. He was searching in desperation for a true God, because he did not want to accept the way that all the redeemers were so unshakably convinced that they were right and at the same time were willing to fight to the death in Jesus' name. Joseph Smith was a nobody until that fateful night of September 21, 1823, when he experienced his strange visions. It then took four years, until September 22, 1827, until God's messenger *Moroni* finally delivered the metal plates to him. Who was this angelic *Moroni*? The son of *Mormon,* and *Mormon* was one of the descendents of the Jaredites who had put out across the ocean all those thousands of years ago. So how could *Moroni,* who in 1827 was already long dead, have appeared to Joseph Smith? Where did the metal plates come from that Smith subsequently discovered in the hill called Cumorah near the village of Manchester in the United States? And which depot did the mysterious metal library—and the other treasures—in far-off Ecuador suddenly come from?

The fact that the metal plates really existed is at least not legally contestable, as 11 other men also attested to their existence in a signed document. In addition to that, the Book of Mormon is filled with such extensive details about family disputes, wars, migrations, genealogies (the sequence of the generations with their countless offshoots), with complicated names, confusing quotes, landscapes and locations and so on, that it seems highly unlikely that a single person could have made it all up during his life. Joseph Smith only lived another 17 years following his visions! As a comparison, the texts of the Old Testament took hundreds of years to compile.

An Alternative Interpretation

For a possible solution to these countless contradictions, I need to dive down into a somewhat fantastic reality:

A group of extraterrestrials refuses to follow the orders of their commander, the "Most High," the "Great Glory" as he is called in the Book of Enoch. That happened thousands of years ago. These extraterrestrials, called "fallen angels" and "watchers of heaven," come down and have their wicked way with the Earth girls and some of them start families. Several names and trades of these beings are known, and they are listed by Enoch. The "Great Glory" causes a flood to come over the Earth—presumably caused by some technological means, such as an H-bomb over a polar ice cap, or the targeted crashing of a meteorite. The group of mutineers recognizes the danger and some of them manage to bring themselves to safety and survive. On Earth a "war of the gods" begins, as it is described in numerous myths and legends. In reality, it is simply a power struggle between the remaining mutineers, because each of them wants a bigger slice of the pie. These survivors—not exactly known for the gentleness of their methods—want to be served. They require minerals, ores, nourishment, and so forth. All the dirty work is done by humans, of course. In their naivety, they believe their bosses to be gods.

"Thou shalt have no other Gods before me!" says the Bible. Priest castes are established; no one may approach "God" lest he be exquisitely clean and offer up sacrifices (nourishment).

The mutineers no longer have access to their high-tech weaponry; it all remains on board the mother ship of the "Most High." However, they can still use their *knowledge.* Nobody can take that away from them. Every single member of the team knows, for instance, how to construct a hot air balloon—as is attested in the Ethiopian *Kebra Negast,* the Book of the Glory of Kings.[57] They all know how a laser works, which chemicals you need to make explosives, or which mixtures of ores result in a durable alloy. And they use this knowledge to impress mankind.

One of these pseudo-gods, or one of his best-trained descendents, has carried out reconnaissance flights and has discovered a distant, uninhabited continent—what we now know as America. He sends a group of his followers there, commanding that they take the ancient metal plates with them. These are the panels upon which the entire history of mankind since the creation— since Adam and Eve—is engraved. This being, called "Lord" by his terrestrial disciples, no longer has the technological wherewithal to transport larger groups of people and their animals as well as a whole bunch of metal plates across the ocean. So he makes them build ships, helping them with technical assistance as and when it occurs to him.

Why bother? What does this "Lord" want with all these metal engravings? And what use is it to him to have a people in America that is not likely to develop advanced technology for thousands of years?

Hold on a minute! There's a contemporary explanation for everything. Whether it's right or not will be confirmed when we read the contents of Ecuador's metal library. The "Lord's" actions are all part of a plan, a thousand-year plan. To digest that a little better, we need to make a little intellectual detour:

How do we warn our descendents in 10,000 years about the dangers of one of our nuclear waste dumps? Around a quarter of a century ago, the

Nuclear Regulatory Commission at the U.S. Department of Energy set up a special committee, the "Human Interference Task Force," specifically to look at this question. Thomas Sebeok, back then one of the world's leading semioticians, recommended placing massive warning signs at the dumps. As nobody is likely to understand today's language in 10,000 years (the time it takes before nuclear waste is safe), the group opted for a communications mix of symbols, graphics, and pictograms. The experts also suggested exploiting the human inclination toward superstition: the plaques also contain cryptic warnings so that the people of the future believe that any ingression onto the sites would be "tantamount to inviting some sort of 'supernatural act of retribution.'"[58] The German periodical *Der Spiegel* noted at the time: "As such warnings tend rather to attract rather than dismay the curious, Sebeok also recommended seeding the ground around the site with the disgusting smell of long-lasting stink bombs."[59] Other researchers in the group suggested using "nuclear sirens" that would give off stored radiation, even in many thousands of years to come. Or a genetically altered cat which, due to the radioactivity, would have a glowing violet-yellow pelt. Myths and tales would transport the message of the "glowing cat" over 10,000 years.[60] Berlin's Professor of Semiotics, Roland Posner, claimed that society needed to be prepared for "future planning at an unprecedented level."[61]

So, what if this is just rehashing an old problem? In January 1980, a gathering of Indio priests and shamans from various parts of the world took place in Montréal, Canada. The representative of the Yanomano tribe from Venezuela reported:

> In the area where my people live, there are many mountains. These are holy places for us. One of them we call "The Bear," another "The Monkey," and a third "The Bird." Long before the white men came, our medicine men regularly made pilgrimages to these mountains. No one else was allowed to visit these sites. The mountains were the source of great power, and the old wise ones of our people spoke of a dangerous material that lay hidden there. Our tradition said that if these mountains were ever destroyed, a great misfortune would fall upon our people.[62]

In the meantime, the Venezuelan government has discovered large deposits of uranium in these very mountains. Where did the wisdom of the Yanomano people come from? Only religions can transport messages over hundreds of generations. And for that very reason, Thomas Sebeok, the head of the "Human Interference Task Force," suggested setting up a kind of atomic priesthood to protect our descendents. Only an elite priesthood or some kind of Masonic committee would be in a position to transmit knowledge down through the generations over thousands of years. Faith, lack of actual knowledge, and an inability to recognize the truth, as well as the constant threat of some kind of divine retribution, would keep the message alive. It's already been proven by our religions today. Non-knowledge, fear, and the priesthood make the unthinkable possible. It's been going on for millennia. We could all be wrong about the origins of our religions. If faith, including the Book of Mormon, is being used as a vehicle to project a message from extraterrestrials into our present age, then we must look forward to new insights. They may be—although it's not necessarily inevitable—quite shocking. It's all a question of viewpoint. We are in the process of trying to convey our warning about the dangers of nuclear waste into the distant future. Why couldn't others, in Enoch's time, have attempted the same thing?

The Inertia of "Common Sense"

We are part of a society of "yes" men (and women). Some agree to everything because of their religious convictions, others because they simply don't know any better, and yet others for purely the opposite reason. No excuse is too outlandish, as long as our feelings of self-esteem are never in danger. We have all prepared something for ourselves and react in a surly manner if anything tries to topple our safe little ivory towers. The very idea of aliens is rejected at the outset because healthy human reason tells us: a) they don't exist, b) if they did they'd be completely different from us, and c) they'd be so far away that they could never reach us anyway. Anyone who thinks that way is just afraid of looking the facts in the eye. Just like the famous quote from scientist Dr. Lee De Forest, who claimed as late as 1957: "Man will never reach the moon, regardless of all future scientific advances."[63] Just 12 years later, on July 20, 1969, Apollo 11 landed on the moon. He wasn't alone. Sir Harold Spencer Jones, the famous British astronomer and head of the Greenwich Royal Observatory, (in)famously claimed that "space travel is bunk" a mere two weeks before the *Sputnik* launch in 1957.

The story of science teaches us that even the most respected minds have backed absurd theories. There are many delightfully amusing books on the subject![64] In the second century before Christ, the famous Alexandrian astronomer Ptolemy taught his students: "I would like to make it clear: the Earth is the center of the universe and all other heavenly bodies revolve around it."[65]

Scientists can contest the errors of their own trade. Science is alive, adaptable, and willing to learn—unlike religion. Religions behave like the proverbial three monkeys: the first covers its eyes, the second covers its ears, the third its mouth. Despite their lack of knowledge, they constantly raise a warning finger. They want to be instructive and well-meaning. Who is there to warn us against well-meaning people?

As a specialist for extraterrestrials I know—no, let me say, I believe—that aliens visited the Earth thousands of years ago. This led to the birth of today's religions and holy scriptures. As we know, every religion in this earthly madhouse claims that *its* holy scriptures are the only true ones. Who—for God's sake!—should we believe? And *what* should we believe in? Most religions prophesy some kind of final judgment. There are religions that announce that the unbelievers will be boiled alive, drowned, beaten down, stabbed, poisoned (with "bitter water"), shot, crushed in earthquakes, or wiped out by some other kind of plague. Luckily, this only applies to the unbelievers—but wait! *Which* unbelievers? Those who don't believe in Catholic dogma? Those who had the misfortune not to be born in Arab or Asian lands, and have never heard either the teachings of Islam or the Hindu faith? Those who were un-lucky enough to grow up in a Christian or other sect? Those who are mem-bers of the Shinto religion in Japan, or those who don't believe in the Book of Mormon or the teachings of Scientology?

Even the most modestly intelligent brain must surely begin to see the problem. The real God, the Great Spirit of Creation, is not responsible for the grand mishmash of earthly religions and dogmas. On the other hand, these religions—along with their holy books—are still around. If we absolve the Great Spirit of Creation from all this—for he would surely be infallible and would never need to make later corrections to any mistakes he might have made, because *he* would never set people at each others' throats or tell every religion that only *they* were right—then who can we blame? The texts are there: the Old Testament, the Torah, the Bible, the Book of Mormon, and many more. As we can hardly hold the creator of the universe responsible for the plethora of holy writings that exist on our planet, then we must surely look for another source to find a halfway acceptable solution to the chaos that exists. The alternative is just to throw all of the holy scriptures into the gar-bage. But that just won't do. Then we would be accusing every prophet from Enoch to Joseph Smith of incessant lying—for they write in the first person, from personal experience. And we would also be ignoring all the technical, medical, and astronomical data in these ancient texts. Dictated directly from some kind of "God" or "Lord." Too embarrassing!

If all these ancient religious texts were inspired, or at least partially in-spired by extraterrestrials, the questions have to be: Where on Earth are they now? Or where off Earth? If the "Lord" of the Book of Mormon was only laying a slow-burning fuse that only thousands of years later was intended to ignite an intellectual explosion, what kind of game was he playing? What did he have to gain? I am far from being the only person who is asking these kinds of questions. In the English-speaking world there are countless publica-tions on the subject. The scientific treatises regarding the ETs' strategies are dominated by professors Bracewell and Deardorff.[66,67,68]

A Human Zoo

There is a hypothesis that claims that the Earth is seen as some kind of refuge by the extraterrestrials, a kind of "zoological garden." The most important precondition for a well-functioning zoo is the well-being of both the keepers and the zoo visitors. So the visitors are forbidden from destroying the nesting sites of rare birds, feeding live dogs to crocodiles, teasing the lions, or removing poisonous snakes. And *all* visitors are required to abide by the rules. The animals are only there to be admired and to be studied from a distance. The keepers, for their part, are there to make sure that everyone plays by the rules.

Now in this case, the keepers know that one species is more intelligent than the others. This species—mankind—is capable of philosophical thinking, of abstraction, of creating various cultures and technologies. The keepers also know that it's only a question of time until mankind tries to break out of its zoo. Should they let man break out? Could he be a danger to the keepers and the zoo visitors?

As humans, we do not (yet) know how many galactic civilizations there might be out there. We cannot exclude the possibility that they include aggressive societies. Maybe there are extraterrestrial beings that have a completely different metabolism to us, or have a body structure and lifecycle that is more like an insect. Quite possibly, such a being would not think much of us at all. Perhaps there is even an extremely aggressive, manlike civilization out there that has won in an interstellar war and is in the process of carrying out some kind of expansion policy fueled by this aggression. It's quite plausible that there are aggressive species that selfishly represent the interests of their home planets and each is only interested in expanding their own planet's sphere of influence. Maybe they are looking for gold or uranium. To counteract these kinds of societies, other aliens form a kind of "galactic club," a little like an extraterrestrial United Nations, with a charter that prohibits any extraterrestrial civilization from interfering with the development of any fledgling civilization until that civilization is capable of joining the galactic club under its own power. The keeper and the animals stick together.

But not forever. You can't stop your children from growing up, and you can't stop mankind from striving toward intergalactic travel. The same rules apply to all intelligent life in the universe. However, there is still one hurdle that has to be overcome before the zoo exhibit "man" may be allowed to break out of its cage: it must prove its readiness to act peaceably. And that will never happen as long as dogmatic religions continue to attack the believers of other faiths.

Are we peace-loving? Are we ready to put aside our aggression? Are we capable, despite our different faiths, to work together harmoniously? These questions will be answered sooner or later. The Earth and its entire evolution has never been a closed system. From our very beginnings until far into the future, we are bound up with the evolution of the cosmos. At the moment, we are still in our "zoo" along with our different races and religions, our wildly differing characters and types, and the various other plants and animals that inhabit our planet. This zoo functions simultaneously as a kind of school. If we get through our probationary period in the zoo, we will be ready for contact with the universe. If we don't manage it, then we will probably destroy ourselves and quite possibly the whole zoo in the process. It's a kind of cosmic natural selection. Mankind must survive its zoo by virtue of its own intellect, dialogues, intelligence, and peaceable nature, before the galactic club will reach out its hand to us.

Thus the embargo; the silence of the keepers. It serves both the observation of mankind as a species, as well as to protect the keepers and the zoo visitors from us. But the embargo against "Earth Zoo" is not total. The ETs are allowed to help us make small jumps, inasmuch as we willingly request this help and prove ourselves worthy of it. But how can helping us in small steps be possible, when an embargo clearly says the opposite? And what does that mean to "prove ourselves worthy"? Don't all religions place great value on proving themselves worthy to their saviors?

Radio astronomer Professor Ronald Bracewell, from Stanford University in California, believes that every terrestrial government would initially try to suppress information regarding radio signals from extraterrestrial beings, the reason being that the first government to decode alien signals hopes to use the knowledge they extract to win some sort of advantage over all the others. We are not just talking about military advantages here; there are also sociological, economical, technological, religious, and cultural aspects. Even if alien messages were to be intercepted by private researchers or even enthusiastic solo amateurs, governments and universities would be in a position to denounce the messages as "foolish pranks," "boasts," or "hoaxes," and then slap some kind of security injunction on them. So how can extraterrestrials provide us with help "in small steps" without being stifled at a national level?[69] How can we solve this problem?

Any indoctrination that is to take place "in small steps" needs to be subtle enough to escape detection by any governments or universities to avoid repression. The message from outer space must, on the one hand, be made available to the public, but on the other hand be "not acceptable or plausible"[70] to the military or science. According to age-old tradition, anything that is "not plausible" is labeled as laughable. And anything that is laughable is beneath the attention of government bodies or universities. In our society, religion is considered to be nonscientific; it is a matter of faith. Therefore, messages are encoded in religious texts where they will not be taken seriously by science. Thus, the embargo remains intact and mankind is brought toward awareness in small steps. "At least no faster than mankind is ready to accept any extraterrestrial message," says Professor Bracewell.[71]

The Uncomfortable Truth?

So what's all this got to do with religious scriptures and the Book of Mormon? Everything! These ancient texts already *contain* alien information *and* actions. Now, just imagine that the "Lord" of the Book of Mormon were suddenly to appear in full regalia in his high-tech UFO above a filled football stadium. Or a place of pilgrimage, over a major city, over an Islamic mosque, a Buddhist temple, or the venerable cathedral of the Mormons in Salt Lake City. What would the faithful think? What would the well-established, white-coated scientists stammer when they were suddenly confronted with the reality that everything they had been disseminating on the subject of extra-terrestrial life and the spanning of interstellar distances was pure hogwash? What would the Jews or the Mormons say when their God was suddenly revealed to be an alien? What will go through the heads of all those military men who have invested trillions of dollars of taxpayers' money in defense missiles, interceptors, and radar systems, when an extraterrestrial suddenly turns up under their very noses? How will all those thousands of anthro-pologists and their millions of followers feel when it is revealed to them—with a snap of the fingers, so to speak—that human development is not just the product of evolution, but that there have been targeted, artificial inter-ventions in the human genome? The result would be some kind of mass cultural and religious shock. We simply would not be psychologically pre-pared. An even worse situation would be if the ETs started filling our skies. That would be seen as some kind of aggression. Man typically fears per-ceived aggressors who endanger us or our beloved property or—even worse—threaten to introduce something foreign into our lives. The God shock would be total!

To avoid these kinds of knee-jerk reactions, the action has to be planned carefully and over the course of several thousands of years. Religions make it all possible. Mankind is spoon-fed something "divine," but at a subconscious level, so that it is not noticed until it is absolutely necessary, as soon as techno-logical evolution has reached the required level, for instance, to think in terms of interstellar travel. Those ETs were much more advanced than us, otherwise they would never have managed to cross the light years to reach us in the first place. They know our psyche, our behavior, for they created man in their own image. This does *not* contradict the theory of evolution, as we are only talking about target mutations here. As they know us as well as they know themselves, the path to the stars will be opened slowly, softly, and in a manner appropriate to the current zeitgeist. That, of course, is changeable. We simply receive small nudges occasionally to get our thinking processes going in the right direction—but no major pushes.

As soon as we are capable of explaining the so-called miracles of the gods in technical terms, and are at least partially capable of duplicating them for ourselves, the gods will be comprehensible to us. Technologies that are just a couple of generations away seem "magical" or "miraculous" to us now. How would your great-grandfather react to seeing a holographic projection in his bedroom? He would think he was having a visitation!

Why did the gods of ancient times make it all so complicated? Couldn't they have just explained who they were and what they wanted?

They did! But the following generations, in their psycho-religious mania to provide an explanation for what was in the ancient texts, came up with legendary nonsense. What's more, it simply wasn't possible to conduct conversations with our forefathers about super-high technology. It was clear to the extraterrestrials that the texts would be adapted over the millennia to match the understanding of the age. Yet hidden within the nonsense remained enough of the original sense for later generations to be able to extract the required information. Understand?

> "A great many people think they are thinking when
> they are merely rearranging their prejudices."
>
> (William James, philosopher, 1842–1910)

I am confident that my contemporary analysis of the situation will neither insult nor injure the gods of the past. The insight was the whole point of the thing. But how do we prove it?

The Visitation of Moroni

Joseph Smith, the founder of the Mormon religion, described his vision of the messenger Moroni this way:

> While I was thus in the act of calling upon God, I discovered a light appearing in my room, which continued to increase until the room was lighter than at noonday, when immediately a personage appeared at my bedside, standing in the air, for his feet did not touch the floor.... After this communication, I saw the light in the room begin to gather immediately around the person of him who had been speaking to me, and it continued to do so until the room was again left dark, except just around him....[72]

The same appearance with the same words repeats itself three times as if the same hologram disk was being played back every time. And the voice? Could have been telepathically transmitted or phonetically aimed directly at a point on Joseph Smith's head. The latter is something we can already do today, and the former is being worked on enthusiastically in many laboratories. But why Joseph Smith, and why 1823? He lived in the vicinity of the hill "Cumorah," in which the plates as well as the translator stones *Urim* and *Thummim* had lain hidden for thousands of years. (James Smith said "Convenient to the village of Manchester, Ontario County, New York, stands a hill of considerable size, and the most elevated of any in the neighborhood. On the west side of this hill, not far from the top, under a stone of considerable size, lay the plates, deposited in a stone box."[73]) The technology had long been hidden in this hill. Joseph Smith had probably passed it dozens of times, and his mental state—as a result of his search for God—made him receptive to the message. The few plates that he found in the stone chest could never have contained the entire Book of Mormon; it is simply too extensive. But think back, dear reader, to the Book of Adam preserved in a sapphire that I mentioned in the first chapter. Do you remember how Seth carried on dialogs with this book? The translator stones, *Urim* and *Thummim,* could have had a similar function. They contained the recordings and served as a playback device. The played the text of the Book of Mormon directly into the head of the awestruck and deeply impressed young Joseph Smith.

I can already hear the protests of the faithful, crying out "Sacrilege!" Gently does it, dear critics from the world of religion. Your scriptures remain fundamentally correct and basically confirm the knowledge of your spiritual community. The content of the Book of Mormon is thoroughly true—with a few later insertions. But the modern interpretation does change the perception of the "Lord." He it was who had the metal plates *specially made for the people of the future*. And what's more, the "Lord" does not reveal himself as a being of spirit. Let's go back to the Book of Mormon:

> *(Ether 3:6) And the veil was taken from off the eyes of the brother of Jared, and he saw the finger of the Lord; and it was as the finger of a man, like unto flesh and blood.... (3:8) And he saith unto the Lord: I saw the finger of the Lord, and I feared lest he should smite me; for I knew not that the Lord had flesh and blood. (3:9) And the Lord said unto him: Because of thy faith thou hast seen that I shall take upon me flesh and blood; and never has man come before me with such exceeding faith as thou hast; for were it not so ye could not have seen my finger. Sawest thou more than this?.... (3:15) Seest thou that ye are created after mine own image? Yea, even as all men were created in the beginning after mine own image.*[74]

Astonishing. The "Lord" possesses a human form and asks the man if he has seen more than a finger. An omniscient god should have known the answer to that one already. He presents himself in a corporeal form, but could, he assures us, also take on a spiritual one (even Moses in the Bible never actually saw his God, but was permitted to look in his direction). Okay. So why, for heaven's sake, can't this "Lord" be the Great Spirit of Creation?

1. He uses technology: shipbuilding, luminous stones, talking balls, a compass, metal plates.

2. The "Lord" takes a trip to America to "correct" his own religion because it has developed in the wrong direction (the mighty old church of Christianity is described a "great whore" in the Book of Mormon).

The Great Spirit of Creation, timeless and omnipresent as he is, would hardly have need of corrections, and he certainly wouldn't renege on his contracts. (In the Old Testament, he made two eternal contracts with Noah and with Abraham.)

Magnificent Temples

On their way from South America into the North, the ancestors of today's Mormons built many temples. This is written in the Book of Mormon. Even temples "after the manner of the temple of Solomon." One of these incomprehensible systems lays high in the Andes in Peru: the temple of *Chavín de Huántar*. No archeologist has a clue who built this impressive temple complex at an elevation of around 3,180 meters above sea level, so they speak respectfully of a "Chavín culture." Even the dating of the building work is uncertain. Experts argue that *Chavín de Huántar*, was a place of pilgrimage, the religious center of an unknown people that suddenly appeared in the high valley of the Mosna River and dominated the culture in the area for several centuries. A center of pilgrimage? Which god did the Indios make pilgrimages to? In *Chavín de Huántar* there are many inexplicable columns and fantastic reliefs featuring flying deities. Below the temple, on the main square, a colleague of the archeologist Julio C. Tello found an obelisk, which now resides in the Archeological Museum of Lima. As no one has ever figured it out, I'll show you the engravings on page 165.

May the light of decryption shine on you! Just as inexplicable is the Raimondi Stela, also found in *Chavín de Huántar* and also to be found in the Archeological Museum of Lima.

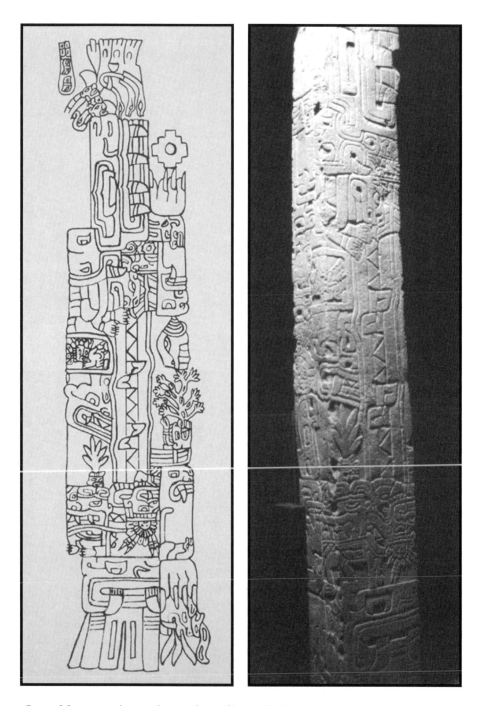

One of the mysterious columns from Chavín de Huántar.

Yet another intricately carved stone block from Chavín de Huántar.

*A close-up of the Raimondi Stela showing the intricate and
precise detail of the carving.*

Engineer Wolfgang Volkrodt believed that the Raimondi Stela
depicted an ancient steam engine.

The block is made of diorite, a type of igneous rock, is 1.75 meters tall, and is 17 centimeters thick. Archeologists speculate about a "jaguar god," "snake or cat gods," "scepters, monsters, masks," and even "the consummate image of the incarnation of the godhead, the god of creation Viracocha."[75] Wolfgang Volkrodt, a top engineer, is the only person who has taken a different approach. He took an extensive look at the Raimondi Stela and was able to clearly demonstrate that the engravings were actually "a highly precise, symmetrical, technical drawing."[76] It perfectly shows the structure of a steam engine with "ratchet blades, rotary pistons, levers, leaf springs, and ball joints."[77] The machine could be used to tighten ropes and pull loads.

Engineers look at things with different eyes archeologists. They have a different reservoir of specialist knowledge. And even though Volkrodt's analysis is faultless and can be attested down to the smallest detail, that doesn't bother the archeologists in the slightest. Their blinkers allow no other interpretation apart from their own. Books by authors such as Volkrodt or Blumrich, a NASA chief engineer who carried out a flawless and word-for-word analysis of the spaceship described by the prophet Ezekiel in the Old Testament,[78] are not considered part of the scholarly literature to be used in their craft. Yet works such as those by Volkrodt and Blumrich pleasantly add another dimension to this cramped and inhibited world view. They open windows and let in fresh thoughts. But keep your eyes firmly bolted shut! What you don't know can't hurt you!

Annoyingly, the winged beings and the engravings on the Raimondi Stela are so finely wrought and precisely carved into the extremely hard diorite that standard tools, such as a sharp chisel, could not possibly have been used. Even a lay observer can see that straight away. That's why I'm showing you the pictures. To achieve this level of precision, extremely hard rotary drills must have been used. Who had that sort of technical expertise back then? My money is on a group of people led by a highly adept "Lord" who provided his people with technology when they needed it, not only to carve diorite with this degree of precision, but also to accurately engrave metal plates.

And I recommend to the industrious Mormons, who are always looking for copies of the metal library of their forefather, that they try taking measurements under the temple of *Chavín de Huántar.*

A Question of Faith

I have great respect for the Book of Mormon and the knowledge contained within it, and I also admire the Mormon faith in the histories of *Ether* and *Nephi*—but there is one point where I take exception. Again and again in the Book of Mormon you can find insertions from (allegedly) Jesus, the (alleged) founder of Christianity. The Church of Jesus, so says the "Lord" in the Book of Mormon, is not developing as had been foreseen; it is evolving in a completely false direction, therefore he, the son of God, has to come to America to found a new true church, the Church of Jesus of Latter-day Saints. I can understand these insertions. Joseph Smith and his brave companions were under a great deal of pressure in the United States. The only religion that was allowed to exist—albeit in countless different variations—was Christianity, and the utterly nonconformist messages of *Ether* and *Nephi* simply didn't fit the picture. Smith and his followers would have been hunted down, denigrated, humiliated, and harassed. Many young Mormons actually did end up in prison—including Joseph Smith himself. Some form of correction was vital, and namely one that brought the son of God, Jesus, into play. So, in came the insertions. Their reasoning was fully understandable, but false (just as false as the later Jesus insertions in the Book of Enoch, which were made by a later hand and exist nowhere in the original text).

The whole Jesus story, starting with original sin, the immaculate conception, the redemption, the resurrection, and going right on through to the ascension—all pillars of the Christian faith—is mixed up from the very beginning. This is not know-it-all Erich von Däniken speaking; this comes from renowned theology professors, such as the Catholic scholars Professor H. Küng and Professor J. Drewermann,[79, 80] or the researcher and church critic Karlheinz Deschner.[81] If, however, the Christian church is based on an erroneous foundation—if there was no original sin and subsequently no need for redemption—then logically speaking no son of God could have come to America to improve and correct his own religion. *Errare humanum est,* as the ancient Romans used to say. To err is human—not divine.

Why a metal library in Ecuador? After the "Lord" patently failed to manifest in any form as the Great Spirit of Creation for thousands of years, and because he used technology instead of miracles, he assumes the burden of proof. In the future! He wants to prove to mankind, in no uncertain terms, that he was the one who was pulling the strings back then. This could work in a critical society that doubts everything, that fakes pictures using computers, that no longer believes in wonders, and that has renounced the supernatural and has bought into scientific reason, but never with new pseudo-miracles (especially miracles that are likely to be exposed after 20 years or so when technology has caught up). Mankind demands solid, scientific, flawless *material* proof. It must be tangible, photographable, datable, and definitively significant. It must be, as the Book of Mormon puts it, "of great value." Not for the people all those thousands of years ago—we are the people being addressed. This conclusion is clearly logical since the "Lord" had the plates engraved all those millennia ago just so they could be read in the future. These proofs of the "Lord" are supposed to turn up "when it shall be said that miracles are done away; and it shall come even as if one should speak from the dead" (Mormon 8:16).[82]

With the metal library in Ecuador, we are standing directly before this great realization.

At the most, we can speculate about the motivation for this "divine" behavior. But the messages themselves are completely unmistakable. The "Lord" of antiquity is not identical with the Great Spirit of Creation. He, of course, would not make any mistakes in the first place, so would have no need of later corrections. So this "Lord" has metal plates specially made for the people of the future, because he wants to prove that it was he who was pulling the strings. The Great Spirit of Creation doesn't need to prove anything.

It seems to me that these so-called gods of the past were—even then—already planning their return, and they wanted to ensure that we will respect them for what they did for us back then. They created us "in their image."

(Mormon 8:14 ff) And blessed be he that shall bring this thing to light; for it shall be brought out of darkness unto light...and whoso shall bring it [the historical account] to light, him will the Lord bless.[83]

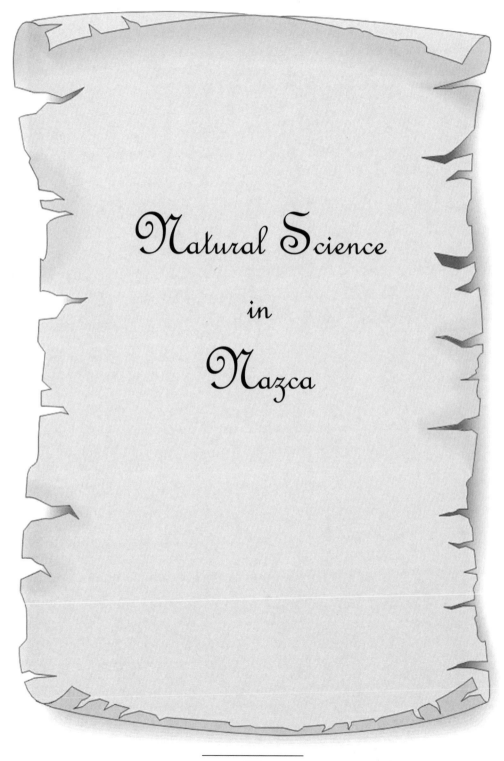

Natural Science

in

Nazca

Back to Peru

"The secret of Nazca has finally been revealed!" announced the headline in one of Germany's most highly respected newspapers, *Frankfurter Allgemeine Zeitung,* on July 14, 2007.[1] The subtitle added: "Geoglyphs in the desert—not for aliens, but for religious processions." Needless to say, I got my share: "It has primarily been the UFO theories of archeo-fantasist Erich von Däniken that have kept the kilometer-long lines and animal figures, features that were scraped into the desert floor thousands of years ago, in the public eye."[2]

Well, at least they gave me that much. The article reveals that the Peruvian archeologist Johny Isla believed he had finally found the solution to the enigmatic trenches. They are, he claimed, ancient procession routes. This had been unequivocally confirmed by a team of Swiss, German, and Peruvian archeologists. Together with Markus Reindel of the German Archeological Institute, Johny Isla had put together an interdisciplinary team of experts to investigate the phenomenon. Markus Reindel presented the results later at the Bonn Center for Science in Germany.

Fabulous. Yet another case of the "most plausible solution" making all further investigation unnecessary. The world is safe again. Hallelujah! But as German lyrical poet Wilhelm Busch once wrote, "But here, as usual, it'll turn out differently from what we expect." Let's take a look at the facts:

There was once a sleepy little town, somewhere behind the seven mountains, in the South of Peru. It was linked to the capital, Lima, by a long dusty road that no one took unless they absolutely had to. This road stretched out for hundreds of kilometers through a desolate desert of sand and gravel and on down towards Chile. Every 90 minutes or so, you would pass a poverty-stricken village: always at a point where an arroyo or stream flowed down from the distant Andes trying to find its way to the Pacific Ocean.

These days, around half of this stretch of road between Lima and Nazca—around 500 kilometers apart—is a paved four-lane highway that winds its way through the desert between the desiccated hills. The once-sleepy town of Nazca has become a lively little place with a museum, a small park, shops, and two banks. Hotels of various differing standards vie to attract tourists, and out on the outskirts of the town there is a desert airstrip with a tower and a bar. From here, visitors can—for around $150—take a flight over the world-famous "Pampa de Nazca." Many of them find it hard to keep down their lunch when the pilot banks from one tight curve into the next.

Down below the airplane, the greatest picture book in the world stretches out across the landscape. Suddenly, a colossal spider appears down on the surface of the rust-brown sand and gravel desert. Then a hummingbird, a monkey, several spirals, a fish, and—between them all—perfectly straight lines, stretching out for miles! There are also various other figures on the mountainsides, including a man who looks more than a little like an astronaut. And then there are "las pistas." They look like rundown, disused landing strips whose contours are just visible through the sand. The longest one stretches out for almost three kilometers.

What on Earth is all this? What is Nazca? Well, for one thing, Nazca is enigmatic, mysterious, and more than a little spooky. The desert in Nazca seems normal enough, yet, at the same time a little eerie. It is magical, beguiling, logical, and yet absurd. Nazca is like a hundred lightning strikes against common sense. If eyes could scream, they'd do it in Nazca. The message of Nazca is veiled and hidden from sight, resisting any attempt at explanation. Anyone who thinks that there could a simple solution for this mystery, probably still believes in the Easter Bunny, too. The landscape is fathomless and irresolvable, preposterous, and senseless. In Nazca, the cords of logic go up in smoke, because they no longer want to be drawn around in circles. Nazca escapes all ingenuity, although year upon year, archeo-criminologists appear there in hordes claiming to have finally solved the mystery. Science—in Nazca it's archeology—compulsively attempts to impose our contemporary knowledge and thinking upon ancient civilizations that had a completely different view of the world.

Brimming with our own self-importance, we claim to be clever, wise, and blessed with an acuity of mind that we do not, in reality, possess. We believe that scientific methodology will lead us inevitably to the nirvana of insight. Thus, over the last few decades, countless Nazca theories, Nazca speculations, Nazca flights of fancy, and plain Nazca nonsense have come about. And in the end, none of them can really provide a definitive answer. Nazca is like a time machine that takes us back into our past, and anyone who wants to get a little closer to solving the Nazca mystery needs to think out of the box. Admittedly, the archeological approach does throw up a few interesting possibilities, but only half-truths.

An Amazing Discovery

In the spring of 1927, Peruvian archeologist Toribio Mejía Xesspe was working in a small tributary valley of the Rio de Nazca. He clambered up the side of the valley and, while taking a bit of a break, looked down onto the pampa. He saw something that looked quite strange: there, in the brown-black desert below, he could see unswerving lines stretching out into the distance in front of him. Yet it wasn't until 13 years later, after he had paced off two of the strange lines, that he finally wrote about his findings.[3]

In June 1940, New York–based historian Paul Kosok took off in a sport plane over Nazca. He sighted several pistas, "líneas" (the smaller, narrower lines), and spirals. His article on the subject wasn't published until 1947.[4]

By then, German geographer and mathematician Dr. Maria Reiche had made her way from Dresden to Peru. Dr. Reiche knew nothing about the lines in Nazca; she was more interested in researching the calendrical connections between the various solar observation sites that can be found in Peru. By a lucky coincidence, she met up with Paul Kosok, who enthusiastically told her about the strange markings he had discovered from the air. Maria Reiche began to look into the subject. At first it was only a side project, but soon she fell prey to the fascination of these strange markings. Together with Paul Kosok, she published a long article about the plateau in the journal *Archaeology.*[5]

In the following years, Maria Reiche got really stuck in Nazca. Her research into the desert plateau became her life, and she spent many years trying to crack the Nazca nut. Back then, even Maria Reiche compared some of the pistas to airstrips: "Then the air passenger...will discover large triangles and squares with lines so accurately flanking the paler background surfaces they look as if they were drawn with a ruler...you might think some of them were landing strips."[6]

When I wrote something along the same lines in 1967—at a time when Dr. Reiche's self-published book was not yet available—I was torn to pieces by the critics.[7] Since then, all sorts of quotes on the subject have been attributed to me—in every imaginable medium—that I never even said. Ironically, it was some of the allegedly "serious" publications that spread some of most ridiculous rubbish that you can imagine. It is a perfect example of how a statement can be falsely quoted and then make its way into the press archive from which it is continuously dug out anew to be misquoted again.

In addition to that, many people assert—regrettably even scientific publications—in a tone of honest indignation, that I had claimed that the Nazca plateau was some kind of "landing site for space vessels."[8] None of these word butchers has ever read my books,[9,10] especially my Nazca book *Zeichen für die Ewigkeit.*[11] If they had done so and had still come out with the usual untruths, I would have had to accuse the authors of lying. As it is, one author simply copies the mistakes of another and adds his or her own two cents worth in the process. That is why, I'm sorry to say, I can't take any of these so-called scientific authors writing about Nazca seriously anymore.

Dr. Maria Reiche didn't find the answer to the Nazca puzzle. Just before she died in 1998, the venerable old researcher bitterly opined that maybe Nazca had something to do shamans or spirits.

There are more theories about Nazca than there are fish in the sea, it seems. I listed as many as I could in my Nazca book, so I'll skip the bibliography here and go straight to a list of some of the more popular theories.

Nazca is:

▶ An astronomical calendar.

▶ Tribal signs of the Indios.

▶ A water god cult.

▶ A mountain god cult.

▶ An agricultural cult.

▶ Agricultural land allotments.

▶ Border markings.

▶ Pens for animals.

▶ Paths for sacred activities.

▶ Procession routes.

▶ Geometrical information.

▶ A site for ceremonial activities.

▶ Copies of visions.

▶ A colossal weaving factory.

▶ A map.

▶ A cultural atlas.

▶ A pre-Inca Olympic games.

▶ A prehistoric balloon launching pad.

▶ An orgy of all kinds of cults.

The Trouble With Archeologists

As you can see, the archeologists have been busy in Nazca. Every couple of years or so, the scientific literature trumpets its latest definitive solution. So we have to ask ourselves: what are they actually doing up there, these archeologists and their sweating students?

Well, they do what archeologists always do: they dig. It's scientifically flawless work and the participating teams, mostly just a handful of people, consist of upright and honest men and women. They look at the layers of stone, bones, remnants of buildings, textiles, pottery, and wood. They gallantly collect, sort, compare, and date every single piece. Finally, they make their conclusions. These come usually from the expedition leaders, who have generally walked the straight path from classical archeological thinking right into the chaotic confusion of Nazca.

Archeologists live from debris. Their view is the world of evolution, always one thing neatly after the other. On the basis of a few tiny fragments, they make their conclusions and apply them to the entire broad plateaus of Nazca and Palpa. Any further questions are unnecessary and unwanted; doubts are ridiculed. Students have no chance against the monolithic immutability of professorial wisdom. Half-knowledge is promoted to the definitive established wisdom that the next generation of students has to swallow. And, before you know it, all of the opinions follow the same pattern, from scientist to journalist.

What can we do to break this pattern? Luckily, there are scientists with measuring apparatus who believe in their readings and not in ideologies. I knew that Professor Gunter Reppchen from the HTW Dresden (a university of technology and economics) had already taken measurements in Nazca in the middle of the Nineties. Professor Reppchen is head of the surveying and cartography department, and his department had been drawn toward Nazca because Dr. Maria Reiche was also a native of Dresden. The scientists from the university aimed to survey all of the geoglyphs and lines in the entire Nazca area to create a digital model.

Professor Reppchen and I met for the first time at his college in Dresden while it was in the process of organizing an exhibition on Nazca. This sober academic, who has also carried out research in the Antarctic, doesn't think much of the idea of aliens, but does attach a great deal of importance to hard (that is, measurable and verifiable) data. At later meetings, I asked him if his department might be interested in carrying out a research project in Nazca that was light years away from standard archeology. In the end, I dug out a number of excellent photographs from my Nazca archive—I have more than 5,000—and began to mark certain areas with a red marker pen. Then I asked questions that no archeologist would have asked (because he would consider them to be superfluous)—questions such as these:

1. Do the narrow zigzag lines, which can be seen in the photograph, really run under the pista, or is it an optical illusion?

2. Do the narrow, roughly 1-meter-wide lines consist of the same material as the pistas, or is it just scraped-off surface material?

3. Is it possible to ascertain whether there is any difference between the magnetic fields of the pistas, líneas, and surrounding gravel, particularly at the crossing points and in comparison with the untouched desert?

4. Are there any anomalies in the conductivity of the ground in comparison with the pistas and the surrounding area?

5. Is there any detectable radiation?

6. Can any material be detected that would not normally be expected in such quantities, such as minerals, ores, gold, or mica?

7. Are there differences in the ages of the various pistas, especially at crossing points?

And so on. All of my questions referred to things that could be precisely measured by science. Professor Reppchen quickly realized that this would involve an interdisciplinary research team and that a Peruvian university would have to be involved. The Nazca plateau is a UNESCO World Heritage Site, which means that no one is allowed to just wander onto it, not to mention start poking around and taking measurements. Over the next few months, a network of scientists stated taking shape, comprised of experts from a number of different universities, every single one of them a specilist in his or her own field. At the head of the pack was the brilliant Dr. Kerstin Hartsch, an extremely gifted geologist who enjoys tackling unconventional problems.

The research project was commissioned by the Erich von Däniken Foundation, which took over all the financing. The HTW Dresden teamed up with the Pontificia Universidad Católica del Perú (PUCP). The most decisive issue involved getting permits to even visit Nazca. These permits were issued—partially, thanks to the help of the German Embassy—by the Instituto Nacional de Cultura (INC). During the entire fieldwork, a representative of the INC, as well as an archeologist from the Universidad Nacional Mayor de San Marcos in Lima, accompanied our party. The two tireless scientists, Reppchen and Hartsch, traveled to Peru many times to help put the various pieces of the puzzle together. It involved tracking down expensive, high-tech measuring instruments, customs permits, negotiations with various institutes and academics, and even banal matters such as finding accommodations for students.

The strange thing is this: nobody had ever thought to carry out magnetic measurements in Nazca before, not to mention geochemical studies or geoelectrical surveying. To start with, the team investigated the surface of the desert. They needed to find out which elements and minerals were normal for the area. In what is known as "hamadas" (areas covered in fine grain sand that has been blown in or away) they discovered manganese, potassium, copper, gold, and—often near to the excavated drawings—clay: the raw materials for ceramics. But nothing out of the ordinary.

Sliced-Off Mountain

In the desert area of Nazca, you can also see a strange-looking mountain, which I called the "sliced-off mountain." Geologists see it differently, of course. I say "sliced-off" because it has no peak, just a flat top, which doesn't fit in with any of the other mountains that surround it. These all end in a point, as you would expect mountains to do. In addition to this, the surface of the "sliced-off mountain" features a zigzag line that can easily be recognized from the air. This mountain with the zigzag line under its pista interested me in particular. It didn't fit in with the general orgy of cults. At the southern end of the pista, on this very mountain, archeologists had discovered small constructions with stone walls. These were categorized—as seems to be usual—as some kind of ceremonial sites. Of all the sites in Nazca, this was one of the most important, but unfortunately the interdisciplinary team had not been able to acquire a permit to work there. German archeologist Markus Reindel from Bonn, the very same man who in the summer of 2007 had triumphantly announced that the Nazca lines were processional routes, had prohibited any measurements. You have to ask yourself: what was his motive for doing so? A team of German scientists came to Peru. They were working together with the Universidad Católica in Lima and a representative of the Instituto Nacional de Cultura, and were just carrying out measurements on the plateau. *And* they had permits. And although these measurements were completely harmless to the site and would not cause damage to the ground or any architectural remnants, a German archeologist prohibited the work. Was he afraid of what might be measured there?

Luckily, my questions didn't apply exclusively to the "sliced-off mountain," and the international research team simply chose a different start site. Were there irregularities in the area, particularly in and around the pistas? The amount of geoelectricity you would expect to find is dependent on the ground's ability to conduct electricity. In a steamy bathroom, it's pretty easy to get a lethal electric shock. But in a dry desert, you would expect the conductivity to be pretty low. To measure the geoelectricity sensors are pushed into the ground, where they give out light pulses of alternating current. The electrodes are moved along the ground profile, step by step, to measure changes in the electrical resistance. Depending on the distance between the electrodes, the electrical resistance can be measured up to a depth of several meters. And this is where we found our first irregularities.

Normally, it's practically impossible to carry out measurements like these in the desert because of the extreme aridity of the ground and the associated difficulty of feeding electricity into the ground at all. But thanks to the newly developed equipment that the team had, and against all expectations, we achieved good and highly detailed results. They discovered that the geoelectrical resistance of the normal ground was relatively low when compared to the geoglyphs. Suddenly—this happened at the end of one of the pistas as well as one of the líneas—the measurements shot off the scale, exceeding the normal values *by a factor of more than a thousand.* You can see it in the dark areas of the tables. There were strips in a patch of ground designated as "Area N4," where an extremely high electrical resistance could be measured running up to and along the edge of the pista. In the "Pampa del Calendario" the center of electrical resistance lay two meters below the surface. Strong electrical anomalies were also measured at other locations. The reason for these is unknown.

But wait—the story gets better. I had asked about the magnetic fields at certain locations. The basis for geomagnetic measurements is the Earth's own magnetic field. To carry out measurements you need a cesium magnetometer. The results from Nazca showed significant differences between the various líneas and the untouched ground surrounding them. Back on the "Pampa del Calendario," the team discovered a veritable network of magnetic anomalies within one of the pistas. The white spots on the picture represent these wild concentrations of magnetic impossibilities. These were so crazy that the measurement apparatus were no longer able to display the values—they were right off the scale! Confusing.

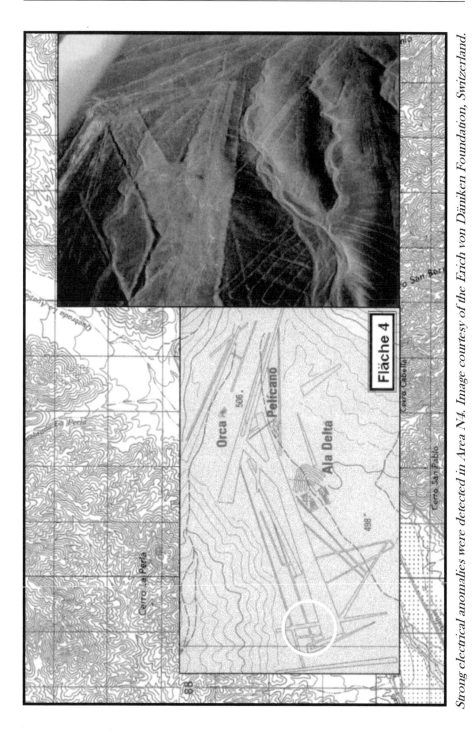

Strong electrical anomalies were detected in Area N4. Image courtesy of the Erich von Däniken Foundation, Switzerland.

Within the survey site "Area P2" (Sacramento), new electrical anomalies cropped up on and below the zigzag lines. Although archeologist Dr. Reindel had forbidden any measurements to be taken on the "sliced-off mountain," the interdisciplinary team did at least manage to obtain readings from two spots. Near the zigzag line, right at the end of the South-West side, electrical anomalies were discovered that exactly matched the zigzag line itself. Really? Nothing special in Nazca? Just a bunch of processional routes?

The pista that resembles the landing strip on the top of the "sliced-off mountain" doesn't cover the entire plateau. On both sides of the pista are margins that are intersected at numerous locations by the zigzag lines. The corners of these zigzags lay where the ground has broken away. There are also furrows of rubble, which have been caused by the rare but heavy rains. Logically, the rain must have run directly over the zigzag lines to create the river along the edge of the plateau which drew the rubble with it. The pictures show it clearly. Why—for holy Atahualpa's sake!—weren't the zigzags washed away as well?

The erosion channels that run from the edges of plateau into the depths are more than a meter wide. It must have rained cats and dogs and elephants! On this "sliced-off mountain," with its pista and zigzag lines, where the water collected before tumbling down into the valley below, there should have been nothing to see but erosion debris. The pictures show the opposite. What's more, the team was able to measure crystal clear magnetic anomalies here too. At the end (or is it the beginning?) of the pista a small rectangular building was discovered around 2 meters wide and a little more than 3 meters long. At the time of the archeological discovery, the remaining walls were about 92 centimeters tall. According to cult thinking, this can only have been a holy place: a place where the pilgrims came or where the priests carried out ceremonies. Why doesn't anybody ask the question: *what kind of ceremonies?* And the additional question: *why here at the start (or end?) of the pista, of all places?* What was so interesting here that they needed or wanted to observe?

Not Quite What They Seem

While I'm at it, I'd like to clear up another piece of nonsense that you can read in all the scientific literature—namely, that it would have been quite simple to construct the líneas and pistas. The fact is, they claim, the sun has been beating down on this desert for hundreds of thousands of years and therefore the surface is a darker brown than the underlying layer. All you have to do is scrape away a few stones or a bit of sand and—presto!—the lighter layer appears.[12,13] There are indeed certain places where that works; I've tried it myself. But at other locations, it's simply inconceivable. If the "sliced-off mountain" had come about by a simple process of scraping away the surface layer, then the zigzag line, which runs *under* the pista, must have been scraped away as well. The boundary ridges that run along each side of the pista would have to have the same color. But they don't. Still think they're procession routes?

Both in and around Nazca things are not quite as natural as they should be, or as the smooth-talking scientists would have us believe. If you recall, I also posed the question as to the age of the pistas in the "Pampa San Ignacio" (Area P5). This is a site where two pistas run into each other and overlap at one end. The research team was able to confirm that the pista that appears on the left of the photograph on page 188 is much older than the one on the right.

This result only tells us that one of them is older than the other, not how old they actually are. Yet the entire Nazca cult—or perhaps we should say cargo cult (= imitation cult)—must be much older than the archeologists claim anyway. Why? Because many of the pistas and líneas on the surface are practically no longer discernible, but lie underneath the surface of the grit.

Nothing unusual in Nazca? What about the chemical elements? As expected, the research team found all the usual components. But when it came to arsenic, the dials went off the scale. The arsenic concentration at some measurement sites was between 10 and 17 times as high as it should have been.

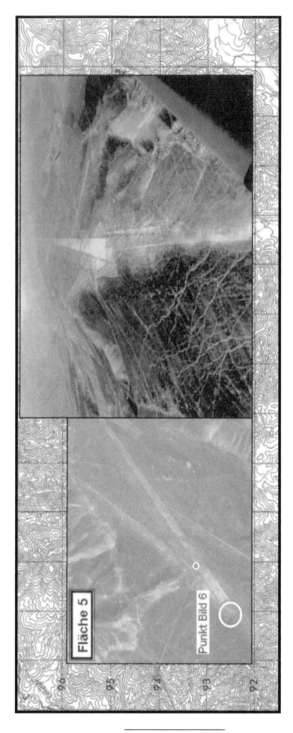

Area P5. The pista on the left is far older than the one on the right.
Image courtesy of the Erich von Däniken Foundation, Switzerland.

The stuff is extremely poisonous! Why would anyone want to use arsenic? Today, it is mixed with lead alloys to improve their consistency. It is also used in semiconductor technology and electronics where, in the form of gallium arsenide, it plays an important role in the manufacture of high-frequency components such as integrated circuits and computer wafers. Arsenic also features in light and laser diodes.

The concentration of arsenic at the measurement points was clearly far too high. It didn't fit in with the general averages of the other elements in the Nazca/Palpa area.

Geologist Dr. Kerstin Hartsch also noticed something else interesting. Directly on the *Panamericana*—the highway that runs from Lima down into Chile, right across the Nazca plateau—between the brown masses of rubble, a number of light-colored layers could be seen. They were particularly apparent on the Sacramento heights and behind the small school in Ilipata. What were they? During my first visit to Nazca, I scratched away at the white substance, which reminded me of salt, using a pocket knife and took it back to my hotel where I tried to dissolve it in hot and cold water. No dice. The scientists carried out an analysis revealing that it consisted of 70 percent of some amorphous material, without any traces of clay. A further analysis using a scanning electron microscope revealed glass-like structures of a kind that only normally occurs when the raw material is rapidly cooled from an extremely high temperature. How is that possible? There are no mysteries in Nazca?

The German-Peruvian research team finally put together their findings in a scientific report, which made the following conclusions:

1. The results of the magnetic measurements showed a clear difference between the líneas and pistas and the untouched surrounding area.

2. The geoelectrical measurements revealed clear anomalies at up to 2 meters below the geoglyphs.

3. The geological environment of Nazca/Palpa is characterized by unusually high, localized deposits of arsenic.

4. A white material was discovered next to certain screes that consisted mainly of glass. The origin of this material could not be explained.

How simple and uncomplicated the world is from an archeological point of view! Nothing mysterious? Nothing unexplained? Thousands of years ago, the inhabitants of the area built huge procession routes to honor their gods. Okay! I've got nothing against that theory. Procession routes did exist! But— and it's a big "but"—the best of the pistas in Nazca and Palpa start and finish in the middle of nowhere. Where are the trails that would have to have led up to these procession routes? Did the faithful fly up there? Hardly. How did the procession route manage to run, straight as an arrow, up the mountainside? And what kind of gods were they worshipping? For what kind of gods do you scratch symbols in the ground that are—with only a few exceptions!—only visible from the air? Do you get the picture now?

The pistas are only visible from the air. So who was supposed to see them?

Those who are not acquainted with ancient Indian literature, in which various kinds of flying vehicles—known as *Vimanas*—are described; those who know nothing of King Solomon's flying chariot; those who haven't got a clue about the shuttle craft explicitly described by Ezekiel; those who have never heard of the Tibetan "pearls in the sky" or the Egyptian "barges of the gods," should wait before they make any final judgment about Nazca.[14] Nobody should be making final judgments about such a wonderful and mysterious place as Nazca; sooner or later they are all revealed to be preposterous. Finally, just to hammer it in a bit more for those who still haven't cottoned on: I never wrote in any of my books that aliens built the "landing strips" in Nazca, or that the site is some kind of "spaceport"!

"Those who cannot attack the thought, instead attack the thinker."

(Paul Valéry, 1871-1945)

Afterword

Dear Readers,

Just to round off, I'd like to tell you about the Archaeology, Astronautics & SETI Research Association (or **AAS**, for short). We are looking for new answers, because the old ones just don't cut the mustard.

Our aim is to find recognized evidence of the existence of a visitation to earth by extraterrestrial beings at some time during man's early history. We want to do this within the framework of established scientific methods, but without letting ourselves be intimidated or limited by existing dogmas or paradigms.

Every two months, we publish the magazine *LEGENDARY TIMES*, which is sent out to all AAS members. We also organize national and international conferences and meetings, as well as study trips to interesting archeological sites.

Our yearly subscription is around $40 (as of this writing in 2009). Our membership includes renowned scientists, as well as laypersons from all kinds of professions.

I would be happy to provide you with further information. Just drop a line to the following address:

A.A.S. R.A.

P.O. Box 6400

Oceanside, CA 92052-6400

USA

Fax : ++1 (760) 941-9150

E-mail: help@legendarytimes.com

www.legendarytimes.com

Chapter

Notes

Mysterious Books

1. "Das geheimste Buch der Welt."
2. Kennedy and Churchill, *The Voynich Manuscript.*
3. Voynich, "A Preliminary Sketch."
4. Gawsewitch, *Le Code Voynich.*
5. Bacon, *Epistola de Secretis,* Chapter 4.
6. Ibid.
7. Geiles, "Spuren der Luftfahrt im alten China."
8. Ibid.
9. Ibid.
10. Ibid.
11. Laufer, *The Prehistory of Aviation.*
12. Ibid.
13. Kanjilal, "Vimana in Ancient India."
14. Bezold, *Kebra Negast.*
15. Kulke, *Geheime Botschaften.*
16. Kennedy and Churchill, *The Voynich Manuscript.*
17. Ibid.
18. Delitzsch, *Die große Täuschung.*
19. Pauwels and Bergier, *L'homme eternal.*
20. Lechtman, "Vorkolumbianische Oberflächenveredelung."
21. Plato, *Phaedrus.*
22. Berdyczewski, *Die Sagen der Juden.*
23. Oberg, *New Earths.*
24. Berdyczewski, *Die Sagen der Juden.*
25. Ibid.
26. Ibid.
27. Ibid.
28. Ibid.
29. Ibid.
30. Ibid.
31. Ibid.

32. Eisenmenger, *Entdecktes Judentum.*

33. Bergmann, *Die Legenden der Juden.*

34. For a digital version of *Babyloniaca,* go to *www.archive.org/stream/babyloniaca05pariuoft*

35. Aram, *Magie und Zauberei.*

36. Grünwedel, *Mythologie des Buddhismus.*

37. Wahrmund, *Diodor's von Sicilien.*

38. Ibid.

39. *Holy Bible.* Used by permission of Zondervan. All rights reserved.

40. Al-Makrizi, *Das Pyramidenkapital.*

41. Schmökel, "Die Himmelfahrt."

42. Ibid.

43. Ibid.

44. Kautzsch, *Die Apokryphen.*

45. Messel, *Der Menschensohn.*

46. Hoffmann, *Das sogenannte hebräische Henochbuch.*

47. Ibid.

48. Riessler, *Altjüdisches Schrifttum.*

49. Ebermann, *Sagen der Technik.*

50. Schott, *Das Gilgamesh-Epos.*

51. Bopp, *Ardschunas Reise.*

52. Blavatsky, *The Secret Doctrine.*

53. Roy, *The Mahabharata.*

54. Hoffmann, *Das sogenannte hebräische Henochbuch.*

55. All from Kautzsch, *Die Apokryphen.*

56. Ibid.

57. Bonwetsch, *Das sogenannte slawische Henochbuch.*

58. Roy, *The Mahabharata.*

59. Ibid.

60. Ibid.

61. Kautzsch, *Die Apokryphen.*

62. Ibid.

63. Ibid.

64. Al-Makrizi, *Das Pyramidenkapital.*
65. Ibid.
66. Ibid.
67. Yoshimura, et al., *Non-Destructive Pyramid Investigation.*
68. Däniken, *Der jüngste Tag.* Final chapter.
69. Kautzsch, *Die Apokryphen.*
70. Fuchs, *Das Leben Adams.*
71. Ibid.
72. *Holy Bible.* Used by permission of Zondervan. All rights reserved.
73. Agrest, "The Historical Evidence."
74. Kautzsch, *Die Apokryphen.*
75. Ibid.
76. Ibid.
77. Ibid.
78. Ibid.
79. Ibid.
80. Ibid.
81. Bonwetsch, *Das sogenannte slawische Henochbuch.*
82. Ibid.
83. Ibid.
84. Kautzsch, *Die Apokryphen.*
85. Ibid.
86. Ibid.
87. Ibid.
88. Ibid.
89. Yoshimura, et al., *Non-Destructive Pyramid Investigation.*
90. Däniken, *Der Götter-Schock.*
91. Kautzsch, *Die Apokryphen.*
92. Ibid.
93. Ibid.
94. Ibid.
95. Ibid.
96. Ibid.

97. Ibid.

98. Hoerner and Schaifers, *Meyers Handbuch.*

99. Kautzsch, *Die Apokryphen.*

100. Kanjilal, *Vimana in Ancient India.*

101. Burrows, *More Light on the Dead Sea Scrolls.*

102. Bonwetsch, *Das sogenannte slawische Henochbuch.*

103. Ibid.

104. Ibid.

105. Kautzsch, *Die Apokryphen.*

106. Ibid.

107. Ibid.

108. Ibid.

109. Ibid.

110. Bonwetsch, *Das sogenannte slawische Henochbuch.*

111. Kautzsch, *Die Apokryphen.*

112. Bonwetsch, *Das sogenannte slawische Henochbuch.*

113. Ibid.

114. Berdyczewski, *Die Sagen der Juden.*

115. Ibid.

116. Ibid.

117. Ibid.

118. Ibid.

119. Apelt, *Platon, sämtliche Werke.*

120. Gaius Plinius Secundus, *Die Naturgeschichte.*

121. Apelt, *Platon, sämtliche Werke.*

122. Ibid.

123. Ibid.

124. Ibid.

125. Ibid.

126. Bürgin, *Geheimakte Archäologie.*

127. Bürgin, *Rätsel der Archäologie.*

128. Landmann, "Das so genannte Voynich-Manuskript."

129. Aram, *Magic and Sorcery.*

Debunking the Debunkers

1. Däniken, *Aussaat und Kosmos.*
2. Blinkhorn, "Un verdadero Mundo subterraneo."
3. "Wir fanden die Wiege."
4. The Book of Mormon.
5. Ibid.
6. Lambert and Millard, Atra-Hasis.
7. Sitchin, *The 12th Planet.*
8. Cordan, *Das Buch des Rates Popol Vuh.*
9. Honoré, *Ich fand den weißen Gott.*
10. Falconi L., Dr. Gustavo. Escritura. Protocolización de la Denuncia. Otorgada por Presentada por el Señor Juan Moricz, July 21, 1969. From the author's archive (Archive No. 0232).
11. Utz Utermann letter to Mr. Erwin Barth von Wehrenalp, ECON Verlag Düsseldorf, October 7, 1972. From the author's archive (Archive No. 0238/ECON documentation).
12. Erich von Däniken letter to Mr. Blumenschein, editor at *Stern* magazine, Hamburg, September 17, 1972. From the author's archive (Archive No. 0238/ECON documentation).
13. Dr. Gerardo Peña Matheus letter to Erich von Däniken, September 12, 1972. From the author's archive (Archive No. 0238/ECON documentation).
14. Pia Buob (Eigenvasenstraße 14) letter to Erich von Däniken, October 22, 1972. From the author's archive.
15. Erwin Barth von Wehrenalp (ECON Verlag, Düsseldorf) letter to Professor Udo Oberem (University of Bonn), September 27, 1972. From the author's archive (Archive No. 0238/ECON documentation).
16. Udo Oberem letter to Erwin Barth von Wehrenalp, October 12, 1972. From the author's archive (Archive No. 0238/ECON documentation).
17. Erwin Barth von Wehrenalp letter to Ramón Burneo, October 6, 1972. From the author's archive (Archive No. 0238/ECON documentation).
18. Ramón Burneo letter to Erwin Barth von Wehrenalp, October 18, 1972. From the author's archive (Archive No. 0238/ECON documentation).
19. Erich von Däniken letter to Dr. Peña, November 11, 1972. From the author's archive (Archive No. 0238/ECON documentation).

20. Erich von Däniken letter to Dr. Peña, December 29, 1972. From the author's archive (Archive No. 0238/ECON documentation).

21. Erich von Däniken letter to Erwin Barth von Wehrenalp, January 7, 1973. From the author's archive (Archive No. 0238/ECON documentation).

22. Dr. Gerardo Peña Matheus letter to Erich von Däniken, January 26, 1973. From the author's archive (Archive No. 0238/ECON documentation).

23. Document of the members of the "Expedición 1969." Signed by all participants. From the author's archive (Archive No. 0232).

24. Erich von Däniken letter to Dr. Peña, February 1, 1973. From the author's archive (Archive No. 0238/ECON documentation).

25. James B. Mobley (Media Associates Company, Los Angeles, California) letter to Erich von Däniken, March 5, 1973. From the author's archive (Archive No. 0238/ECON documentation).

26. Erich von Däniken letter to Dr. Peña, March 16, 1973. From the author's archive (Archive No. 0238/ECON documentation).

27. Thompson, Ron. "The Mystery of Ecuador's Secret Treasure." Newspaper article from June 17, 1973. From the author's archive (Archive No. 0095).

28. "Juan Moricz realizaria una nueva expedición."

29. "Pueden tildarme de loco" (and various other articles from the author's archive; Archive No. 02699).

30. Erich von Däniken letter to Neil Armstrong (Cincinnati), February 18, 1977. From the author's archive (Archive No. 01752).

31. Neil Armstrong letter to Erich von Däniken, February 24, 1977. From the author's archive (Archive No. 01752).

32. "Auf den Spuren."

33. Däniken, *In Search of Ancient Gods.*

34. Ibid.

35. Kaufhold, *Von den Göttern.*

36. Professor Gebhardt letter to Erich von Däniken, November 29, 1972. From the author's archive.

37. Lechtmann, "Vorkolumbianische Oberflächenveredelung."

38. Berlitz, *Geheimnisse.*

39. Borges, "La Cueva de los Tayos."

40. Various expeditions, described by various authors in: Boletín Histórico. Pupl. Del Órgano de la Dirección de Historia y Geografía Militares del Estado Mayor Conjunto de la FF.AA. Ecuadoriano, Año 1, No. 3, Julio 1977, as well as further issues of the same bulletin. (From the author's archive; Archive No. 03149.)

41. Hall, Stan. *Tayos Gold. The Archives of Atlantis.* 2005. Available from *orders@booksurge.com.*

42. Ibid.

43. See *www.goldlibrary.com.*

44. The Book of Mormon.

45. Ibid.

46. Ibid.

47. Ibid.

48. Ibid.

49. Ibid.

50. Ibid.

51. Ibid.

52. Ibid.

53. Ibid.

54. Ibid.

55. Ibid.

56. From the Vatican Website: *http://212.77.1.245/news_services/bulletin/news/20586.php?index=20586&lang=en#TESTO%20IN%20LINGUA%20INGLESE*

57. Bezold, *Kebra Negast.*

58. Sebeok, *I Think I Am a Verb.*

59. "Stinkbomben in Atomlagen."

60. "Atomzeitalter."

61. Posner, *Warnungen.*

62. "Indianer prophezeien."

63. As quoted in the *New York Times* on February 25, 1957.

64. Cerf and Navasky, *The Experts.*

65. Ptolemy, *Almagest.*

66. Bracewell, *The Galactic Club.*

67. Deardorff, "Examination."

68. Deardorff, "Possible Extraterrestrial."
69. Bracewell, *The Galactic Club.*
70. Deardorff, "Possible Extraterrestrial."
71. Bracewell, *The Galactic Club.*
72. The Book of Mormon.
73. *scriptures.lds.org/en/js_h/1.*
74. The Book of Mormon.
75. Wedemeyer, *Sonnengott.*
76. Volkrodt, *Es war ganz anders.*
77. Ibid.
78. Blumrich, *The Spaceships.*
79. Kung, *Unfehlbar?* (and numerous other books by the same author).
80. Drewermann, *Der sechste Tag.*
81. Deschner, *Das Kreuz* (and numerous other books by the same author).
82. The Book of Mormon.
83. Ibid.

Natural Science in Nazca

1. Prganatz, "Das Gehimnis."
2. Mejía Xesspe, *Acueductos y caminas,* pp. 559-569.
3. Ibid.
4. Kosok, "The Mysterious Markings."
5. Kosok and Reiche, "Ancient Drawings."
6. Reiche, *Geheimnis der Wüste.*
7. Däniken, *Erinnerungen.*
8. Légare, *Les Lignes de Nazca.*
9. Däniken, *In Search of Ancient Gods.*
10. Däniken, *Habe ich mich geirrt?.*
11. Däniken, *Zeichen für die Ewigkeit.*
12. Kern, et al (referring to Maria Reiche): Peruainische Erdzeichen.
13. Silvermann, "Beyond the Pampa," pp. 435-56.
14. See also Däniken, *The Gods Were Astronauts,* and Blumrich, *The Spaceships of Ezekiel.*

Bibliography

Note: The book titles listed are the English versions (where available). Otherwise a translation of the title has usually been offered (in italics in parentheses following the original language).

Agrest, Matest M. "The Historical Evidence of Paleocontacts." *Ancient Skies, volume 20, no. 6,* 1994.

Al-Makrizi. *Das Pyramidenkapital in al-Makrizis,Hitat. (The Pyramid Chapter in al-Maqrizi's Khitat.)* Translated by E. Graefe. Leipzig: Hinrichs, 1911.

Apelt, Otto. *Platon: sämtliche Werke. (Plato: complete dialogs.) Volume VII, Laws.* Hamburg: Meiner, 1988.

Aram, Kurt. *Magie und Zauberei in der alten Welt. (Magic and Sorcery in the Ancient World.)* Berlin: Deutsche Buch-Gemeinschaft, 1927.

"Atomzeitalter." *("Atomic Age.") Spiegel Special,* no. 61, 1995.

"Auf den Spuren nach dem Wesen vom anderen Stern." *("On the Trail of the Being from Another Star.") Westdeutsche Allgemeinen Zeitung,* October 20, 1982.

Bacon, Roger. *Epistola de Secretis Operibus Artis et Naturae et de Nullitate Magiae. Opera Johannis Dee Londoniensis e pluribus exemplaribus castigata olim et ad sensum integrum restituta...* Ex Bibliopolio Frobeniano, Hamburg: 1618.

Berdyczewski, Micha Josef (Bin Gorion). *Die Sagen der Juden von der Urzeit (The Ancient Legends of the Jews).* Frankfurt am Main: Rutten & Loening, 1913.

Bergmann, Judah. *Die Legenden der Juden. (The Legends of the Jews.)* Berlin: C.A. Schwetschke & Sohn, 1919.

Berlitz, Charles. *Geheimnisse versunkener Welten.* (Originally titled *Mysteries From Forgotten Worlds.)* Frankfurt: Societäts-Verlag, 1973.

Bezold, Carl (Ed.). *Kebra Negast, die Heiligkeit der Könige. Abhandlungen der philosophisch-philologischen Klasse der Königlich-Bayerischen Akademie der Wissenschaften (Kebra Negast, the Book of the Glory of Kings. Essays from the philosophical-philological class at the Royal Bavarian Academy of Sciences).* Volume 23, Section 1. Munich: Verlag der königlichen Akademie, 1905.

Blavatsky, Helena. *The Secret Doctrine, Vol. 1.* London: The Theosophical Publishing Company Ltd., 1888.

Blinkhorn, Jorge E. "Un verdadero Mundo subterraneo en America." *El Telégrafo,* September 28, 1969.

Blumrich, Josef. *The Spaceships of Ezekiel.* New York: Corgi, 1974.

Bonwetsch, Nathanael. *Gottlieb: Die Bücher der Geheimnisse Henochs: Das sogenannte slawische Henochbuch (The Slavonic Book of Enoch).* Leipzig: J.C. Hinrichs, 1922.

The Book of Mormon, 16th Edition. Church of Jesus Christ of Latter-Day Saints. 1966.

Bopp, Franz. *Ardschunas Reise zu Indras Himmel. (Arjuna's journey to Indra's heaven.)* Berlin: Königliche Akademie der Wissenschaften, 1824.

Borges, Alberto. "La Cueva de los Tayos. Entrada a una civilización Subterraneo." *("The Tayos Cave. Gateway to a subterranean civilization.")* *Vistazo,* July 1976.

Bracewell, Robert Newbold. *The Galactic Club: Intelligent Life in Outer Space.* San Francisco: W.H. Freeman & Company, 1975.

Bürgin, Luc. *Geheimakte Archäologie. (The Secret Files of Archeology.)* Munich: Herbig Verlag, 1998.

——. *Rätsel der Archäologie. (Mysteries of Archeology.)* Munich: Herbig Verlag, 2003.

Burrows, Millar. *More Light on the Dead Sea Scrolls: New Scrolls and New Interpretations.* New York: Viking Press, 1958.

Cerf, Christopher, and Victor Navasky. *The Experts Speak.* New York: Pantheon, 1984.

Cordan, Wolfgang. *Das Buch des Rates Popol Vuh–Schöpfungsmythos und Wanderung der Quiché-Maya. (The Book of Councillor Popol Vuh–The Creation Mythology and Migration of the Quiché Mayans.)* Düsseldorf: Diederichs Verlag, 1962.

Däniken, Erich von. *Aussaat und Kosmos (The Gold of the Gods).* Düsseldorf: Econ Verlag, 1972.

——. *Erinnerungen an die Zukunft.* (Published in English as *Chariots of the Gods.*) Düsseldorf: Econ Verlag, 1968.

——. *The Gods and Their Grand Design.* New York: Putnam, 1984.

——. *Der Götter-Schock. (The God Shock.)* Munich: Bertelsmann Verlag, 1992.

——. *The Gods Were Astronauts.* New York/London: Element Books, 2002.

——. *Habe ich mich geirrt? (Did I get it wrong?)* Munich: Goldmann Wilhelm GmbH, 1985.

——. *Der jüngste Tag hat längst begonnen. (Judgment Day Has Already Begun.)* Munich: Goldmann, 1995.

———. *In Search of Ancient Gods.* New York: Putnam, 1973.

———. *Zeichen für die Ewigkeit.* (Published in English as *The Arrival of the Gods.*) Munich: Goldmann Wilhelm GmbH, 1997.

Deardorff, James W. "Examination of the Embargo Hypothesis as an Explanation for the Great Silence." *Journal of the British Interplanetary Society, 40,* 1987.

———. "Possible Extraterrestrial Strategy for Earth." *Quarterly Journal of the Royal Astronomical Society, No. 27.* Published for the Royal Astronomical Society by Blackwell Scientific Publications, Oxford, 1986.

Delitzsch, Friedrich. *Die große Täuschung. (The Big Deception.)* Stuttgart: Deutsche Verlags-Anstalt, 1921.

Deschner, Karlheinz. *Das Kreuz mit der Kirche. (The Cross the Church Must Bear.)* Düsseldorf: Econ Verlag, 1974.

Drewermann, Eugen. *Der sechste Tag. Die Herkunft des Menschen und die Frage nach Gott. (The Sixth Day. The Origin of Man and the Search for God.)* Zurich: Walter, 1998.

Ebermann, Oskar. *Sagen der Technik. (Legends of Technology.)* Leipzig: Hegel & Schade, 1931.

Eisenmenger, Johann Andreas. *Entdecktes Judenthum. (Judaism Unmasked.)* Königsberg: n.p., 1711.

Fuchs, C. "Das Leben Adams und Evas." *("The Life of Adam and Eve.") Die Apokryphen und Pseudoepigraphen des Alten Testaments (The Apocrypha and Pseudoepigrapha of the Old Testament), Volume II.* Hildesheim: Olms, 1962.

Gaius Plinius Secundus. *Die Naturgeschichte. (Naturalis Historia.) Volume 1.* Translated by Prof. Dr. G.C. Wittstein. Leipzig: Gressner & Schramm, 1881.

Gawsewitch, Jean-Claude. *Le Code Voynich.* Self-published, 2005. Available at the Beinecke Rare Book and Manuscript Library, Yale University.

"Das geheimste Buch der Welt." *("The most secret book in the world.") P.M.* [Peter Moosleitners] *magazine,* February 2007.

Geiles, Herbert. "Spuren der Luftfahrt im alten China." *("References to Aviation in Ancient China.") Astronomische Zeitschrift, Issue 9,* 1917.

Grünwedel, Albert. *Mythologie des Buddhismus in Tibet und in der Mongolei. (The Mythology of Buddhism in Tibet and Mongolia).* Leipzig: F.A. Brockhaus, 1900.

Hall, Stan. *Tayos Gold. The Archives of Atlantis.* Kempton, Ill.: Adventures Unlimited Press, 2005.

Hoerner S., and K. Schaifers (Eds.) *Meyers Handbuch über das Weltall. (Meyer's Handbook of Space.)* Mannheim: Bibliographisches Institut, 1964.

Hoffmann, Helmut. *Das sogenannte hebräische Henochbuch. (The Hebrew Book of Enoch).* Bonn: P. Hanstein, 1984.

Holy Bible. New International Version. Copyright 1973, 1978, 1984, International Bible Society.

Honoré, Pierre. *Ich fand den weißen Gott. (I Found the White God.)* Frankfurt: Scheffler, 1965.

"Indianer prophezeien den Untergang des weißen Mannes." *("Indians Foretell the Downfall of the White Man.")* Weser-Kurier, January 21, 1980.

"Juan Moricz realizaria una nueva expedición a Cueva de los Tayos." *El Universo*, August 3, 1976.

Kanjilal, Dileep Kumar. "Vimana in Ancient India: Aeroplanes Or Flying Machines in Ancient India." Extract in Erich von Däniken, *Habe ich mich geirrt? (Did I get it wrong?).* Munich: Goldmann Wilhelm GmbH, 1985.

——. *Vimana in Ancient India.* Calcutta: Sanskrit Pustak Bhandar, 1985.

Kaufhold, Peter. *Von den Göttern verlassen. (Left by the Gods.)* Recklinghausen: Meyster, 1983.

Kautzsch, Emil. *Die Apokryphen und Pseudoepigraphen des Alten Testaments. (The Apocrypha and Pseudoepigrapha of the Old Testament.)* Volumes I and II. Freiburg/Leipzig: J.C.B. Mohr (Paul Siebeck), 1900.

Kennedy, Gerry, and Rob Churchill. *The Voynich Manuscript.* London: Inner Traditions, 2005.

Kern, Hermann, et al. *Peruainische Erdzeichen. (Peruvian Ground Drawings.)* Munich: Kunstraum Munchen e.V., 1974.

Kosok, Paul, and Maria Reiche. "Ancient Drawings on the Desert of Peru." *Archaeology,* Volume II. New York: Archaeological Institute of America, 1949.

——. "The Mysterious Markings of Nazca." *Natural History, volume LVI.* New York: American Museum of Natural History, 1947.

Kulke, Ulli. "Geheime Botschaften aus dem Mittelalter." *("Secret messages from the Middle Ages.")* DIE WELT, March 1, 2007.

Kung, Hans. *Unfehlbar? Eine unerledigte Anfrage. (Infallible? An Unfinished Question.)* Munich/Zurich: Piper, 1989.

Lambert, Wilfred G., and Alan Ralph Millard. *Atra-Hasis, the Babylonian Story of the Flood.* Oxford: Clarendon Press, 1970.

Landmann, Erhard. "Das so genannte Voynich-Manuskript. Eine wissenschaftliche Abhandlung." *("The so-called Voynich manuscript. A scientific treatise.") Magazin 2000plus,* Issue 233.

Laufer, Berthold. "The Prehistory of Aviation." *Field Museum of Natural History, Anthropological Series, Volume XVIII, Number 1,* Chicago Natural History Museum, 1928.

Lechtman, Heather. "Vorkolumbianische Oberflächenveredelung von Metall. *("Pre-Columbian Metal Gilding Techniques.) Spektrum der Wissenschaft,* August 1984.

Légare, Felix. *Les Lignes de Nazca. Trop belles pour être vrais. (The Nazca Lines. Too good to be true.)* Montreal: La Revue Québec Science, 1968.

Mejía Xesspe, Toribio. "Acueductos y caminos antiguos de la hoya del Rio Grande de Nazca." *Actas y Trabajos Científicos del XXVII Congreso 1939,* Volume 1, pp. 559–69. Congreso Internacional de Americanistas, Lima, 1942.

Messel, Nils. *Der Menschensohn in den Bilderreden des Henoch. (The Son of Man in the Similitudes of Enoch.)* Gießen: A. Töpelmann, 1922.

Oberg, James Edward. *New Earths—Restructuring Earth and Other Planets.* New York: New American Library, 1981.

Pauwels, Louis, and Jaques Bergier. *L'homme eternal. (The Eternal Man.)* Paris: Gallimard, 1970.

"Plato. Phaedrus, circa 370 B.C." In *The Dialogues of Plato,* translated by Benjamin Jowett. Oxford: Oxford University Press, 1931.

Posner, Roland. *Warnungen an die ferne Zukunft—Atommüll als Kommunikationsproblem. (Warnings to the Distant Future— Communication Problems Regarding Nuclear Waste.)* Munich: Raben Verlag, 1990.

Prganatz, Hilmar. "Das Gehimnis von Nazca ist gelüftet." *("The secret of Nazca has been revealed.") Frankfurter Allgemeine Zeitung,* Issue no. 161, page 9, July 14, 2007.

Ptolemy. *Almagest.* London: Gerald Duckworth & Co Ltd., 1984.

"Pueden tildarme de loco, pero hay seres superiors bajo la tierra." *El Universo,* August 6, 1976.

Reiche, Maria. *Geheimnis der Wüste. (Mystery on the Desert.)* Self-published. 1968.

Riessler, Paul. *Altjüdisches Schrifttum außerhalb der Bibel. Die Apokalypse des Abraham. (Ancient Jewish Non-Biblical Writings. The Apocalypse of Abraham).* Augsburg: Dr. Benno Filser, 1928.

Roy, Potrap Chandra. *The Mahabharata.* Calcutta: Bharata Press, 1891.

Schmökel, Hartmut. "Die Himmelfahrt Henochs. Neue Aufschlüsse aus Keilschriften." *("Enoch's Ascension. New Information from the Cuneiform Texts.") Frankfurter Allgemeine Zeitung,* Issue number 159, July 12, 1973.

Schott, Albert. *Das Gilgamesh-Epos. (The Epic of Gilgamesh.)* Stuttgart: Reklam, 1977.

Sebeok, Thomas A. *I Think I Am a Verb: More Contributions to the Doctrine of Signs (Topics in Contemporary Semiotics).* New York: Plenum Press, 1986.

Silvermann, Helaine. "Beyond the Pampa: The Geoglyphs in the Valley of Nazca." *National Geographic Research and Exploration 1990,* pp. 435–56. Washington, D.C.: National Geographic Society, 1990.

Sitchin, Zecharia. *The 12th Planet.* New York: Stein & Day, 1976.

"Stinkbomben in Atomlagen." *("Stink bombs in Nuclear Sites.") Der Spiegel, issue no. 51,* 1981.

Volkrodt, Wolfgang. *Es war ganz anders: Die intelligente Technik der Vorzeit. (It Wasn't Like That: The Intelligent Technology of Prehistory.)* Munich: Herbig Verlag, 1991.

Voynich, Wilfrid Michael. "A Preliminary Sketch of the History of the Roger Bacon Cipher Manuscript." *Transactions of the College of Physicians of Philadelphia,* Vol. 43, 1921.

Wahrmund, Adolf. *Diodor's von Sicilien Geschichts-Bibliothek. (Diodorus of Sicily's Library of History.)* Volume 1. Stuttgart: Krais & Hofmann, 1866.

Wedemeyer, Inge von. *Sonnengott und Sonnenmenschen. (Sun God and Sun People.)* Tübingen: Wasmuth, 1970.

"Wir fanden die Wiege der Menschheit." *("We found the cradle of civilization.")* An exclusive report on the "Moricz 1969 Expedition" in *La Plata Ruf,* Buenos Aires, December 1969.

Yoshimura, Sakuji, et al. *Non-destructive Pyramid Investigation by Electromagnetic Wave Method.* Tokyo: Waseda University, 1987.

Index

About the Author

ERICH VON DÄNIKEN was born in Zofingen in Switzerland in 1935. His lifelong fascination with extraterrestrial visitors first found its expression in 1968 with the international bestseller *Chariots of the Gods.* Since then he has become the most widely read nonfiction author in the world. His books have been translated into 28 different languages and have sold more than 63 million copies. In addition to his writing, von Däniken is an ever-present figure on the international lecture circuit; is regularly seen on our screens presenting fascinating documentary films and TV series; is the chairman of A.A.S. R.A. (Archaeology, Astronautics & SETI Research Association) and a regular contributor to its magazine, *Legendary Times*; and somehow still finds time for his family back in Switzerland.